# HOW TO BREAK THE BARRIERS TO SELF-LOVE

## *And Live a Life of Authenticity*

# Table of Contents

# Dedication

I dedicate this book to all the brave souls that have endured the challenges of being human and yet continue to learn, grow and evolve as spiritual beings. It takes great strength, courage, self-compassion and inner wisdom to walk through the darkness to find the higher truth. Many life lessons have caused severe emotional distress that have sadly damaged the most beautiful hearts. The burdens of pain that weighed heavy on these souls have caused them to withdraw their light and question their divine value.

I am grateful that we are waking up together to create a world of authentic formation as we expand into the light of our being and conquer our own inner fears with the wisdom and intelligence of higher consciousness.
We are not on this journey alone. We are all finding our way back to our authentic selves as we meet each challenge with the divine essence of our spirit and spread our love and light into this love-starved world.

We are collectively the game changers, way showers and cycle breakers, changing the old paradigm of fear, greed and control into a world of cooperation, compassion, and unified love consciousness.

Thank you for your service to the world. You are the miracle our ancestors have been praying for.

# Introduction

*"Purpose is not a noun, it is a verb... We experience purpose when we do something that's greater than ourselves. We experience purpose when we push ourselves and grow."*

*~ Aaron Hurst*

We, as human beings, living both a physical and spiritual life on planet earth, can easily become confused about our journey here. It seems as if we long for something that will allow us to feel safe, but at the same time allow our souls to explore the world with vigor, spontaneity, emotional depth and some risk taking to live out our soul's purpose. Somehow, we became locked in between our ego-driven need for security and our desires to live life through the spirit of who we are. Many of life's challenges have caused us to seek healing through spiritual practices to gain the inner peace that was disrupted by external chaos. As we dive into our spiritual practices, we energetically feel a sense of balance and harmony as we realign with our true selves – our energetic body that was born from the All-Loving Creator. The question is, why do we keep getting pulled away from our divine nature by outside forces, causing us to seek spiritual realignment? You may be surprised to find out.

Our spiritual nature is the embodiment of divine love. Divine love is not an emotion - it is consciousness. Before we entered the physical body, we did not know what our true value was. We needed to learn more about our soul's ethereal essence by having a human existence on planet earth. As souls outside of the human structure, we are energetically entwined with all soul bodies sharing unified love. As a collective body of this divine love, we are the most powerful source of light, love and healing energy. It is difficult to understand the value of that deep love because we have nothing to compare it to. To understand the meaning and significance of spiritual unity and embodied love consciousness, we had to experience nonlove and separation. The best way to do that is by having our own unique soul journey in a material world filled with temptation, desire and human emotions that cause us to question love, which then through us into a whirlwind of confusion about our divinity and purpose here on this planet.

During our physical journey, our biggest challenge is to stay connected to the love we embody as souls, while we experience feelings of nonlove through the many negative emotional challenges of the human experience. When situations that feel like nonlove cause us to question our lovability, we experience feelings and emotions that trap us in fear which causes disruptions and malfunctions in our energy body system. This leads to insecurities and a desperate need to find love again. We innately know that love is the answer to our external problems, but we unknowingly kept searching for love outside of ourselves because we lost touch with the spirit within. We are seeking that inner harmony that became tainted by our own fears of not being good enough to exist in this world. Where would we go if the world extinguished us from society due to our inferior nature? How would we survive this threatening annihilation? This is the inquiry of the fearful ego mind that could not exist outside of the third-dimensional human structure. The ego mind becomes the savior as we continue to lose more of true nature and become reliant on our ability to fight for survival. We are fighting for love and security through artificial means because the authentic love that we embody has been blocked by fears of unworthiness.

As we desperately seek love outside of ourselves as a security base in our new world, the fear energy trapped in our soul bodies cause us to attract more fear energy. This is because like attracts like. The more negative energy trapped in our soul bodies, the more we will attract that same energy. As we were birthed into human existence, we were already absorbing negative energies of the people around us who personify fear from their negative earthly experiences. Once you enter the physical plane and are cared for by souls who have energetic pockets of deep emotional pain that keep them stuck in debilitating fear, you are most likely going to feel that energy and create your own fears of non-lovability and unworthiness. When fears become stronger than love, we lose ourselves in the human experience of temptation and desire.

We are being schooled on planet earth to determine our strength and devotion to divine love. When we disconnect from love because negative emotional energies were unknowingly absorbed into our energy bodies early on in physical life, we seek external validation and pleasures that give us a false sense of love, which leads to a false sense of security. We are not being abandoned by love. We have abandoned ourselves when we allowed fear to overtake the love we have within us.

We were sent here to experience what it feels like to be separated from love so we can appreciate divine love. Unfortunately, the fears were so overwhelming that we not only disconnected from love, but we allowed a split from unity consciousness.

We were granted the free will to discover if we have the spiritual strength to defy anything that may weaken our souls, trap us in emotional disharmony, and cause us to deny the existence of universal love and a one mind consciousness. When we are connected to unified love consciousness, the output of our energy is love at its highest vibration. When our souls experience nonlove through difficult earthly experiences, the energy of our souls puts out a low frequency of energy, which is uncomfortable and uneasy not only for our souls, but for those that are affected by this low-level energy. Once we understand how the energy we release into the world affects us and everyone around us, and how others will then affect those they enmesh with, we will allow ourselves to be more aware of our energy output. Even though we are living separate soul journeys to discover our true nature, we are still sharing our energy with all energy bodies in both negative and positive output.

Energy output relates to the thoughts, feelings and emotions we are individually experiencing through our human experiences. Our goal in this physical reality is to learn self-awareness so we can put into action any necessary steps that will bring us back to unity love consciousness if our human experiences cause us to sway from it. Self-awareness means having the ability to recognize and understand one's thoughts, feelings and emotions so any negative energies stemming from them can be healed with the divine love we embody. This will create an energy output of love which can help heal a world where so many people still struggle with the internal fears of nonlove.

We entered this world with the spirit of love. As we learned about who we are in our new world through the people guiding us from the beginning phases of life, we either continued to embody that unity consciousness and learned more about the value of love or we began to experience the fear of nonlove and abandonment. We are being tested on our ability to stay devoted to our divine essence, even when we are being challenged to love who we are. There are many people who are unable to see how they are the ones who have abandoned themselves unknowingly by becoming trapped by the fears of nonlove. There are also many people doing the healing work so they can experience the embodiment of divine love while having this physical experience. This is the final goal of our journey here on planet Earth – to embody divine love even in the darkest times of experiencing nonlove. This is quite a challenge and that is why most of the world lives in fear. The fear was too intimidating and terrifying, so many gave into it without realizing the healing power of love that could conquer this debilitating energy. It all comes down to survival of our physical existence because we have not collectively evolved enough to fully embody the higher truth. The higher truth is that we are divine beings having a human experience to learn the value of self-love and unity love consciousness. There is no departure of our true nature, only the demise of our temporary physical structure that is being utilized to learn this higher truth. There is so much to learn and so much to unlearn on this physical journey because we have been manipulated by fear for an exceedingly long time. If we do not learn to live by the higher truth, the journey will just keep becoming more difficult and challenging for us as human beings.

In the physical body, we learned from an early age that we are individualized and that our caregivers are out there, and we are here in our own body as "me" or "I." This is where we first experienced a separation from all that is. If we are not spiritually supported by those around us, which most of us are not, then we may experience a painful loss of love. This causes us to seek love from another source – the world out there which we believe is separate from ourselves. As we become more reliant on the physical world to hold us in that love space and unification, we begin to question who we are as that love space becomes unreliable and we feel a breakage in connection to those around us. This separation from who we are as spirit and the feelings of disconnect from the world cause debilitating pain for the soul. The human mind takes over and creates protection mechanisms to ensure our safety in what feels like a threat to our existence. The annihilation of our true essence is an illusion, and one that we must dissolve so we can return to the divine truth. It starts with love for the self. We must be able to embody that love energy even though our human experiences have caused us to question our ability to love and be loved.

Due to the many difficult experiences of being human, we have drifted away from our true path. We have unknowingly been led towards self-preservation by the human experience of fear, doubt, and indifference. This is because the people we looked to for guidance had already lost their way. They were not able to stay on their path and learn about the value of love. Instead, they became caught up in the experiences that felt like nonlove and fell into the trap of unworthiness. As they became more preoccupied on proving their value in the world instead of knowing who they are, they became more attached to finding their worth outside of themselves. Their connections to others become one of necessity and survival and no longer one of divine love. They have learned to seek some external savior that is going to take away all their fears and give them a sense of security. Their purpose of learning about the essence and value of self-love was thwarted by their inability to stay on course, learn from earthly experiences and rise above the fears that caused them to question who they are. As their experiences caused them to feel emotional discord instead of authentic love, they no longer found trust in the Creator or within themselves. Instead of learning how to love themselves as their Creator does, they learned how to fight for acceptance in a world filled with judgments, criticisms, and nonlove. Authentic love is love without measure. It has no conditions. It is the essence of who we are. We do not just feel it, we embody it as our truth. When we lost ourselves in the third-dimensional world of judgment, competition, materialism, extremism, and narcissism, we disconnected from the biggest part of ourselves - our soul's essence. We have become disconnected from ourselves and others causing deep pain to the soul because we long for that unity love that seems forever lost.

As our teachers at the beginning phases of life, the primary adults during our growing up years taught us from their internal place of fear instead of self-love. They have fallen prey to the many fears of the world which took them off their path to self-love. Self-love is not just love for oneself. It is a consciousness that is carried within the soul that gets expressed outward into the field of consciousness that we are all intertwined with. Self-love means we see ourselves in that oneness of divine consciousness with others.

When we are fully in self-love, we know who we are and nothing and no one can take it from us. If the grown-ups caring for us were unable to love themselves through their human challenges, then they would not be able to properly guide us on our journey to discover the depths of divine love. Without that spiritual support, we had to learn about self-love through many difficult experiences of nonlove.

The grown-ups that became our teachers also came here from that unity consciousness. This means we are all being greatly challenged, including our primary caregivers and our forgotten ancestors, by the human experiences of fear. Most of us have lost our way because the challenges we face in the physical world are plentiful. We turned against others and ourselves when we fell into the fear trap. This does not mean we all took the wrong direction. We took the direction that was meant to teach us more about the pain of not loving ourselves so we could appreciate the importance of divine love and our connection to all that is created from it.

We lose our way when we cannot get back on the journey to self-love, and instead get stuck in self-rejection and self-sabotage. This does not make us bad human beings. It makes us emotionally unhealthy human beings that took the wrong message from our difficult experiences. We are still learning how to embody self-love. The journey to self-love becomes stagnant when we cannot see our worth through the illusions of fear that we experienced during the physical journey.

What we need now is the spiritual strength to come back to the truth. The truth is that we are infinite beings that exemplify love at its highest level. We were not sent here to struggle. We were sent here to discover more about ourselves through our struggles. If we continue to deny who we are as spiritual beings, then we will not be able to fulfill our mission and discover what it means to exist in oneness and experience this elevated level of love on this physical journey. If we can find our way to the truth while being challenged on this physical plane of existence, then we are on the journey to self-love that ultimately reaches a full and complete expression of who we are.

Self-love is a journey unique to everyone. It does not just happen automatically. It is a process of learning, unlearning, and relearning. We learned from the fear energy surrounding us that we must be validated by the world to be loved. Now we must unlearn the programming that comes from that misguided messaging and relearn the truth about who we are.

We are here to learn about the natural evolution and progression of the soul. We could not learn this outside of the physical body. We needed to learn it by experiencing the disruptive energy within our souls when we do not love, honor and value who we are as divine beings. These disruptive energies cause so much unease within us, which we then project outward into the atmosphere. If we ignore these uncomfortable sensations because we fear they invalidate our worth, then we may unknowingly get too deep into the human experience of fear.

To evolve higher is to understand what divine love is and be able to embody it in our human form so we can bring that higher love to this disconnected world. The more we learn about love during our physical journey, the more we will understand our deeper connection to the All-Loving Creator for which we are all a part of. The more we spread love into the world, the more people we can help through the fears that overwhelmed their souls so they can find their way to self-love. We are on this mission together, although we are all having different experiences to get us to the divine truth. Some of us are learning faster than others. We must remember that we all came from the same source of love. We need to learn about our human worth as well as our spiritual value, so we can do what we came here to do. When we and others have lost the way, we must realize that it is part of our mission to find our way back to self-love.

The way we get pulled away from seeing the truth about self-love is by getting stuck in those human emotions that do not feel comfortable to our souls, causing us to remain stagnant, instead of progressing towards self-love. Human emotions that make us feel bad about ourselves can cause a soul to feel weakened, not enough for the world, and not connected to a love source. Instead of loving ourselves enough to rise above these emotional experiences, we sadly let them take us down.

Many of us are struggling to find our worth. This is because deep within us is the fear of judgment and rejection. At an early age, we learned from the people in our family and social environment who we must be to gain their approval. Just the same, these people have learned from others who they must be to fit into the world. As we have become more disappointed in ourselves and the world we live in, we continuously seek improvement, more spiritual wisdom, and that one miracle that is going to save us from our uncomfortable feelings about who we are.

As humans, we want inner peace, so we are no longer struggling with the thoughts that we are not enough or do not have enough. We want unconditional acceptance and support from a world that seems judgmental and self-focused. We want to be able to love others without getting hurt by them. This has been our biggest human challenge – we do not know how to navigate the journey to self-love with so many fears weighing against us.

Those that cannot tolerate the pain of their dark emotions have found addictive behaviors as a comfort source. They may have completely disengaged from their soul's essence and found temporary comfort in numbing out their negative emotions. Those that have followed a path towards enlightenment without healing their subconscious pain have become addicted to spiritual practices to find that inner peace again. Many times, spiritual practices are used as high-level coping mechanisms because loving ourselves unconditionally is just too difficult. We have yet to find the balance between our need for physical security in a world of uncertainty and the eternal source of love that lives within the depths of our souls.

Spirituality, as it is rooted in the atmosphere of the earth's plain, has become our savior. We are learning who we are through these daily practices of tapping into the inner mind for answers. There are a myriad of books on psychology that address the mental mind and our human need to live a more positive life. There are also many books that discuss the purpose of the soul's journey on planet earth and the need for understanding our spiritual essence. This book will address our human and spiritual needs, and the reason we struggle to see the full value in who we are as we simultaneously experience both realms of existence. We know on one level that we are perfect divine beings, but there is another level within us that denies this truth and keeps us from fully embracing self-love while in human form.

Throughout this book, you will learn how we continue to rely on spiritual practices to bring us back into balance and yet still struggle to love ourselves. In every spiritual book you will read words of comfort and ease that give you an understanding of your worth as a human being with spiritual roots. For you to personify this truth, stand fully in your integrated human and spiritual creation and trust your inner knowing to lead the way, you must acknowledge the truth about the deceptive energies within the human experiences of fear and rejection. These are the energies that trap us, block our inner truth, dim our illuminated essence, and cause us to find our way back through the darkness. We are more intelligent than that. It makes me wonder how we fell into the darkness so deeply and became trapped by its deceptive strength.

We are not meant to step into self-love regardless of our inner fears of unworthiness. We are meant to learn the lessons within our emotionally charged experiences and allow these lessons to guide us to the ultimate truth and divine love. This can only be done with a clearer understanding of the levels of human consciousness, the vibration of the soul, how parts of us have become split off from our wholeness, and the innate wisdom of the spirit within. All of this will be explained in this book to give you a clear understanding of self-love, why we struggle with it, and how to truly embody the essence of our godlike nature.

We read self-help books, engage in spiritual practices, treat ourselves to healing the mind, body, and soul with some of the many ancient healing modalities, and yet we are always seeking more. There seems to be that missing piece that will take us to nirvana, enlightenment, and a total transformation. It is that place where you never question who you are because you know, on a soul level, that you are a miracle of life. We do not know what we are missing; we just feel that there must be more to who we are. What we are not realizing is there is nothing missing, but there is a disconnect somewhere within the whole self. This means we may be experiencing soul loss without our awareness.

We may feel less than whole, although we are always whole. What we do not know is that there are parts of us that have not been fully integrated into ourselves. This is due to the inability to find peace in certain intense emotional situations that caused us to reject the parts of us that are now trapped in their suffering. As we reject these parts, they are pushed outside of our awareness, so we do not have to feel their pain. As innocent beings of divine source, we did not realize how far we strayed from our truth. With each human experience that caused us to question our value, we ventured more into the ego mind to protect ourselves from further rejection.

It has been said by many spiritual gurus that we are souls having a human experience. We are taught that our earthly experiences will help us evolve as spiritual beings. When we overcome an emotional difficulty, we learn a valuable lesson that brings us closer to self-love. The more we learn about self-love, the more we expand our awareness of who we are. We attempt to learn the lessons that are presented before us so that we can grow and reach authentic self-love and enlightenment. Authentic self-love is the highest level of love. It has no barriers. It is the same level of love that our Creator has for us. It does not fluctuate. It does not choose who or what to love. As we embody this authentic self-love, we see all of nature as love. This includes all other living beings, even if they are unable to express love.

Let us not only seek divine truth through superficial means as we hide parts of ourselves from the world. Let us exemplify the essence of our true selves as we learn how to dissolve the false, disempowering, and debilitating thoughts of unworthiness that keep us disconnected from ourselves and others.

As we learn more about who we really are without all the fabricated fluff that feeds the ego-self, we will give the power back to the light within us which keeps us connected to one another through a universal body of eternal love. The more we love ourselves, the more of that love energy we spread into the world where so much fear exists. We are the cure for this love-starved world, but we are just as capable of starving it of love without realizing it. Self-awareness is the first step towards truly embodying that authentic self-love. Our true purpose in this world is to experience the emotions that defy love so we can appreciate the essence of love we are made of. As we learn this, we continue our mission to spread love and peace into the world.

This book is not meant to fill you up with wisdom but is meant to draw out the wisdom that lives within your spirit. May the words in this book flow into your body and shift your soul back into that high frequency of divine love that you aligned with before the human experiences of fear dimmed your light. Every experience that caused you to question your worth and significance in the world has jammed up your nervous system, locked up your energy body and created a distorted reality filled with fear and distress.

We have learned to save ourselves from the experience of rejection by rejecting any parts of ourselves that do not fit into this world. We have become so deeply entrenched in the human experiences that cause pain and fear, that we have lost our ability to trust the journey. For our own safety, we became reliant on others and formed co-dependencies. This caused us to lose more of ourselves and become accustomed to a fabricated self as we learned to adapt to the expectations of others. The inner conflict of our true selves fighting against these false and debilitating narratives is what keeps us on a continuous cycle of confusion.

We have so much inner wisdom waiting to break out and guide us on our journey. Before that wisdom can come through, we will need to release the mind programs that block it. We became stuck in a never-ending chase for safety and validation in the world. We came here to find and experience a deeper truth, and yet it is the biggest challenge of our lives. Every spiritual practice is a reminder of our divine essence. Unfortunately, we need more than that. We need to release the deep fears of unworthiness that we are trying to remedy through spiritual work that does not address the depths of our souls. True spiritual work addresses all levels of our being so we can resolve the conflicts within us.

We need to see the bigger picture around our human experiences. Since we are in the physical world, we have concerns for our physical lives. Anything that threatens our physicality will cause us to question our survivability. When we become frantically focused on safety because of many bad experiences, it is difficult to remember that we are infinite beings and that this journey is meant to help us evolve as souls.

Our goal on this planet is to achieve unity consciousness while we are having a human experience through our individual soul bodies. Self-love is our first step towards unity, but it begins with self-awareness. Without self-awareness to lead us back to loving ourselves, we cannot love the collective consciousness of souls because we are separating ourselves from love.

Enjoy the sacred space within this book. It is here to remind you how human you are, how divinely perfect you are and how much you are loved by your Creator. You are here on this planet to learn the truth about your divine essence and what it is like to be challenged in that truth. Let us not seek the validation of our worth through others, but through our own heart space and essence of our spiritual strength.

# Chapter 1

## Human Consciousness and Brainwave States

*Our greatest human adventure is the evolution of consciousness.
We are in this life to enlarge the soul, liberate the spirit, and light
up the brain.*

*~ Tom Robbins*

On this physical journey, it is important to discover who we are through every human trial, both positive and negative. These experiences produce corresponding emotions, which then feed into our belief system. The negative beliefs that are formed from undesirable memories about our experiences become a part of our consciousness that keep our souls in darkness where we do not see our light. The unhealed emotions attached to these negative beliefs keep the soul's energy from flowing with grace. They cause the ego to take control of our lives so we can feel safe. It is the job of the ego to keep our negative beliefs below our awareness and to distract us with the desires of the material world whenever uncomfortable emotions arise. When the soul becomes overwhelmed with unhealed emotions from negative memories, it cannot experience the physical world from a level of higher consciousness, which defies our true purpose.

To understand this further, let us look at the different levels of the mind and an understanding of human consciousness and our spiritual essence. Human consciousness is not a solid structure and therefore not the brain. Consciousness is the energy of our thoughts, feelings and emotions that express themselves through our personality traits, tendencies, and behaviors. When a thought is accepted by the brain, it then becomes part of the mind. The mind, in its different levels of awareness, becomes consciousness.

The highest level of consciousness is the higher mind. Then there are lower levels of consciousness which act as our navigation system for our physical experience. These levels are known as the conscious mind, the subconscious mind, and the unconscious mind. Lower levels do not mean physical lower levels since the mind is not physical. Lower levels refer to lower levels of consciousness.

The conscious mind is our analytical, logical and rational part of the mind. It is aware of our immediate surroundings in our physical environment. It is also where our ego resides. The conscious mind knows how to plan, strategize, and make logical decisions. It is important to our survival as it has awareness of our surroundings.

The subconscious and unconscious levels of the mind sit below conscious awareness. Their purpose is to store information only, but not to analyze it. These levels of the mind store the information of everything we have experienced in life based on our personal perceptions of each experience. Memories in the subconscious mind are more accessible than memories in the unconscious mind since the unconscious mind contains memories that we have blocked out or repressed. These memories will affect how we react or respond to current life circumstances and how we make important life decisions. Studies have shown that we may also carry memories of our ancestors through our DNA which can also influence our physical lives.

These lower parts of the mind do not know if the information they contain is true or false, or when any of these recorded experiences occurred. They do not register time and cannot distinguish between real or imagined events. The memories in these parts of the mind are playing out in a continuous loop like a recorded movie. Our conscious recollection of these memories will most likely change over time, but the way they were recorded will stay the same until we change our perceptions about these experiences. The way we consciously think about these experiences and the way we perceive them subconsciously are two different things. As an example, suppose you consciously believe your parents did the best they could. In your subconscious mind is a recorded memory of being a child where you perceived they could have done better, but chose not to, and this led to you feeling hurt and unlovable. Now your conscious mind and subconscious are in conflict.

The higher mind is the innermost part of the mind. When the higher mind is in an expanded state, you feel the connection to the universal mind, which is one mind and one consciousness - all that is created by the All-Knowing, All-Loving, Creator. This awareness expands into the body of love consciousness that we are all part of.

Consciousness is energy and energy cannot die. It can only change form. When the physical brain is no longer available due to death, near death experiences, coma states and powerful mystical experiences, we may find ourselves in spiritual energies that feel like home to us. This is because we are remembering who we are on a spiritual level. When we are in the physical body, many times we forget that this planet is a temporary home.

The saying that we are not our bodies is true in that we are above our bodies. We are the consciousness that lives through our bodies. In that consciousness, in its higher mind level, we are in a state of higher love, higher compassion and higher knowing. We feel connected, protected, and divinely held in union with our Creator. When we are blocked from the higher mind due to too much low-level activity in the lower levels of the mind, we start to fear the safety and security of our existence. Low-level activity is low-level thoughts, feelings and emotions that keep us trapped in the fears of not being enough for the physical world. This is where we forget that we are perfect divine beings. We become attached to the physical aspects of our existence, which sometimes cause us to question our value and significance in the world.

It is through these lower levels of consciousness where we begin to worry if we belong here, if we are wanted and loved by the people caring for us and if we are significant enough to be a value to the world. We are seeking assurance of our survival in the physical realm through approval by others. If we have doubts and worries about our worth, we begin to focus intently on ourselves to correct our perceived deficiencies so we can be accepted by others. This is a survival mechanism, and it comes from the physical brain. These survival tactics will be terminated upon death of the physical body since the soul is energy which continues to survive outside of the body.

As children, we are fully dependent on others to keep us safe and alive. Whenever a caregiver, knowingly or unknowingly, causes us to feel bad about who we are, we begin to question if we are enough for them. This leaves us feeling completely vulnerable and afraid of losing our protection in the world due to our own perceived deficiencies. As a coping mechanism, we adapt to the expectations of our caregivers to gain their acceptance. This adaptation takes the form of suppressing the parts of us that we believe our caregivers and others in the world found unacceptable. We then create more acceptable parts of us which, without our knowledge, create what is known as the "false self."

As we suppress more of what we believe are inferior parts of ourselves, we create new parts based on what others expect from us, which causes us to eventually become accustomed to our false self. Over time, we forget who we really are. These newly created so-called acceptable parts are not from our Creator and, therefore, are not a part of our authentic selves, which is divine. These created parts came from the ego part of the conscious mind which is focused on survival. We cannot reach authentic self-love if we are rejecting the parts of us that came from an authentic place, while we cling to these false expressions of who we are as a survival tool.

As an example, suppose as a child you were told or you perceived in some way that your laugh was annoying. To be accepted by others, you suppressed your unique laugh, along with the emotion of sadness related to feelings of rejection. You then created a false version of you that laughs very quietly hoping no one will hear you laugh. This is to avoid further rejection. This false part of you becomes your new "normal" right into your adulthood. You never laugh out loud even though it would have been natural for you to do so. The ego keeps the feelings of sadness suppressed and you believe your quiet laugh is just who you are. By this example, you see that not only do we suppress parts of ourselves to avoid further rejection, but we also suppress any emotions that cause us to feel bad about who we are. This is part of our survival strategy because when we feel bad about who we are, it makes us want to shut down or somehow numb out from the world because it feels like a threat to our well-being. Since we need to interact with the world to survive, we can easily get triggered by anyone that is unkind, judgmental, critical, demanding, untrustworthy, or unreliable because we are already suppressing fears of rejection and feelings of unworthiness. A trigger is anything that causes a person to relive a past emotional trauma, causing them to react as if the trauma was happening in the current moment. Reliving the trauma causes the suppressed emotions to become reactivated and the body responds as if it was under threat. Although you are not experiencing the trauma again, your subconscious mind believes you are.

The ego plays a huge role when it comes to our need for survival by doing its best to keep our emotions suppressed, but what it can't control is the automatic reactions when something in the current environment triggers our deepest fears. This is because the subconscious mind is not in the head but runs through the entire body. Our unhealed suppressed emotions affect our nervous system which goes into an automatic survival reaction and causes the body to find a way to safety by invoking a fight, flight or freeze survival response.

When we go into a fight response (prepare for attack) or flight response (run to safety), blood rushes through parts of our body for strength and speed. When we go into freeze response, we are shutting down the body. We become weakened and unable to move or act against a threat.

Another survival response is known as "fawn." This is common in situations where there is physical abuse. The victim spends their energy trying to please their abuser to avoid conflict. The victim of abuse is working to achieve a connection to dodge defeat.

Whenever we get triggered by a current situation that wakes up a stored emotion, we tend to react to the current situation with the same intense emotions as the past. This is because our bodies suddenly become flooded with emotions that were once dormant. For example, suppose you have a memory of a primary caregiver tossing a shoe at your head with a look of disgust, causing you to feel fear and anger that you have since buried. As an adult, you are at a friend's house and she, in a joking way, tosses her shoe towards you. The emotions of fear and anger immediately surface because the mind is recalling the stored memory, and simultaneously the body is reacting to the fear response through the nervous system. You may get angry even though it was obviously for fun. The anger is the nervous system going into fight response. This automatic behavior is not easy to stop. It is an automatic reaction that seems to be out of your control. This is because it is coming from stored energy in your body. It happens so quickly that you do not have time to evaluate what you are feeling. The emotions of fear and anger have a strong charge to them and, in that moment, become reactivated, leaving no time for your conscious mind to catch up to what is happening.

When we are no longer in a physical body, the higher mind, which we can call spirit, continues to survive as a higher level of consciousness. The conscious part of the mind dissolves when we leave our physical bodies. This means the false self also dissolves as it was a creation of the ego mind. What we take with us after death is the memories stored in the subconscious and unconscious levels of the mind, but without the protection of the ego. This means we have awareness of the pain we buried. These emotions are carried within the soul and do not get left behind. They are part of our karma and need to be healed so they can be released from the soul. Karma is a repeat of actions based our consciousness. It is the driving force of our actions. To heal karma, we need to heal the lower-level thoughts, feelings and emotions that keep us stuck in a negative loop, so we don't continue our negative actions. When we have negative karma, we become attracted to the negative karma of others. When we leave our bodies, we acknowledge how karma played out in our physical lives and work to release the karmic energy from our souls so we can rest in peace. If you believe in past lives, where the soul returns in another physical body to have another physical experience, then that karmic energy will return with the soul which means the soul will continue to experience negative events until there is a positive change in consciousness.

The subconscious and unconscious memories in the lower levels of the mind become merged together after death and continue to live through our attachments to our human life. These attachments are due to feelings of unfinished business during our physical journey. This means the soul cannot fully ascend to a higher plane of existence. It stays in the lower realms, closest to the earth's plain. The soul remains in limbo because it has high and low levels of consciousness that are pulling it in two directions, keeping it stagnant. The soul will get stuck in the lower astral plane until it releases itself from those earthly attachments. This may require forgiveness of others and oneself, release of shame, guilt, anger, or any other low-level frequency that keeps the soul from ascending higher.

The Tibetans have followed the philosophy that we need to resolve our inner confusion before death so we can live a peaceful existence in the spiritual realm. It is said that we do not only need to live well, but we must die well to experience nirvana when we leave our physical bodies. With all the challenges of being human, it may not be that easy to leave this planet with a fully healed consciousness. We have so many stored memories of unpleasant experiences. For us to follow this Tibetan philosophy, we would need to make peace with the memories and negative emotions that were suppressed below our conscious awareness. We would have to become aware of what has been recorded in the subconscious and unconscious levels of the mind and release what makes us feel bad about who we are and the life we lived. If it is true that we would have a more peaceful journey in the afterlife, then it would be to our benefit to delve into those lower levels of the mind. This means giving up the façade of the false self that we created to protect ourselves from feeling unworthy or being rejected. Not only would it give us a more peaceful life while we are still in the physical body but will give us peace when it is time for us to leave this world. To give up the false self, we must learn how to get back to the true self.

While we are having our physical journey, we are learning how to adapt to the world so we can feel safe. This means we will continue to live by our false selves which will not feel good to our soul bodies. Our souls are longing for the connection to ourselves and the unified consciousness of all divine beings. That is where we came from and when we lose connection to it, we feel a sense of deep loss. The challenge is that the ego mind is so strong that it takes control of our physical existence because if we cannot physically survive, neither can the ego. Survival means being accepted in the world. If we feel unaccepted, unloved or unworthy, then the ego will use all its strength and power to bury those feelings and replace them with a more acceptable false self-identity.

Due to so many human experiences that have caused us fear, we are in a battle within ourselves. The ego mind has no knowledge of our divine energy. The ego's job is to show the world that we are good enough to be here. This causes the ego to strive for acceptance in whichever way it can get it. The divine self already knows that we are perfect beings created from the ultimate source of love. When our earthly experiences cause us to feel that we are not worthy of receiving love, the ego steps in to create lovable parts of us so we do not get rejected by the world. These so-called lovable parts are created under the expectations and dictates of our caregivers and society. They are not true parts of us, but we believe they are. As we live through our false selves, we no longer feel a connection to who we really are or where we came from.

When we speak of loving ourselves, we are only speaking of loving our acceptable selves, which could be made up of false parts. Self-love is loving all of ourselves as our Creator made us. The journey we are on is about shedding the false self so we can embody our divine truth and not only live well but die well. This has been a challenge for many of us since the false self gives us a sense of safety and acknowledgement in the world. It takes an extraordinarily strong human mind to drop the façade and let the soul stand naked in its truth without fear of rejection. This is the journey we are on. We are learning how to feel vulnerable and still love who we are, even in a world filled with many demands, judgments, and expectations. This is why self-love is our biggest challenge and our biggest reward.

If we are to fully heal from our disconnected selves, we must first understand the need for the false self and how it can lead us back to who we really are. We came here to learn, and part of that learning is to fall into that ego trap and then learn how to rise out of it and be the human spirit we came here to be. Along this journey are the many lessons that will help us see the divine truth. We were not expected to come to this planet, suffer from feelings of nonlove, and then still love ourselves regardless. We came here to experience the separation from our true selves so we can learn the value of unconditional love. Spiritual gurus are always telling us to love ourselves. In this new-age craze, people are constantly posting memes and affirmations on social media about how we need to love ourselves, but are we fully embodying self-love? It is important that we know we are already on the self-love journey and doing it in small progressive steps. If we are working through the fears we have been collecting since childhood, healing the negative emotions we have trapped in our bodies, and engaging more with the higher mind, then we are on the journey towards the ultimate level of divine truth.

From the moment of conception until this very day that you are reading this book, you have been learning. The idea is to apply the lessons towards self-love, not away from it.

The more we simply try to talk ourselves out of our feelings of unworthiness and fear of nonlove through memes and affirmations, the more we ignore that there are stored memories deep within us that may be feeding us negative thoughts and feelings. Since these levels of the mind are out of conscious awareness, we do not see any reason to worry about them. The problem is that they have a lot of control over us. Creating the false self does not mean these suppressed emotions do not continue to influence the way we live our lives. Although we claim these quotes as a testament to our worthiness, I wonder if we genuinely believe it. These compassionate phrases that affirm our innate value are only words to the ego mind if we are not showing ourselves genuine, unconditional love when life challenges us. When we use these inspiring quotes to provide us with a temporary moment of self-acceptance while we ignore our deep feelings of unworthiness, then we are living from our false self because we are in self-denial.

It seems that since we can pacify our ego mind with these inspiring quotes of our flawless divine nature, we do not do the inner work that can truly lead us back to the higher knowing of who we really are. This makes me wonder if we are truly and fully loving ourselves or are we just trying to escape the darkness through the many spiritual practices we engage in, or the self-love quotes we take ownership of.

The truth is that we are loving ourselves naturally and effortlessly, but not all of ourselves. We are limited in the love we feel towards ourselves because there are parts of us that we believe are undeserving of love. We believe that these are flawed parts of us, so we rejected them to ensure our acceptance and safety in the world. We abandoned these parts of ourselves when we feared that they were the cause of a disconnect with our loved ones. This means we may be carrying feelings of unworthiness that are suppressed deep within us. Even if we felt we had a good and safe childhood, there were most likely times that we questioned if we were good enough for those we needed love from.

As humans, we operate under different and fluctuating brainwave states. Brainwaves are different frequencies within the brain. All our thoughts, emotions and behaviors are a result of communicating neurons within the brain. The frequency or speed these neurons communicate determines their brainwave state. The human brain contains billions of neurons which connect and communicate with each other using electrical currents and a network of brain circuitry. When neurons are activated, they send out electrical pulses which create a brainwave state. The brainwave state affects our state of consciousness.

At birth and until about the age of two years, children are mostly in a sleep state, known as the delta brainwave state and function primarily from the subconscious mind. Although these young children are unable to respond well to their environment, their perceptions of their outer world are being downloaded into their subconscious minds.

From age two to about the age of six years, the child begins to connect more with their environment and form their perceptions about it based on their imagination. At this age, they still do not have the cognitive abilities for critical thinking and function mostly from a meditative or hypnotic state known as the theta brainwave state. In this brainwave state, the child is highly suggestible to their outer world, meaning what they take in through their senses becomes their inner reality and eventually becomes part of their belief system. They believe what they are told about who they are and the world they live in, which many times are based on the thoughts, beliefs and opinions of others and not truth or fact.

From about the age of six to eight years, the child moves into an alpha brainwave state where their cognitive abilities strengthen. They begin to form judgments about their environment, but still tend to use their imagination more than logic to interpret their environment. As children develop more of their cognitive functions, they operate more from a beta brainwave state. This is when the children become more focused and can think more logically and critically about themselves and their environment. Their thinking processes, however, will be greatly influenced by what has already been downloaded into their subconscious mind during their earlier years when the brainwave states lacked logic and understanding. This means they already have a strong belief system that is not based on critical thinking abilities, but only on the imagination and what they believed to be true based on what others have taught them. These beliefs will be relied upon for the life of the child unless they change them, which is not always an easy task. The same holds true for those that influenced the minds of these small children. They too were operating from a belief system that may go back to their young childhood. In this regard, people are passing on beliefs systems that were born from the imaginative child mind that is mainly focused on safety and getting their needs met. This is why so many people are unknowingly living from survival consciousness which keeps them from exploring their full potential.

Numerous studies indicate that we navigate our lives about 5-10% from conscious awareness and about 90-95% from the lower levels of consciousness. The adult sometimes operates from the immature child mind because the subconscious mind reacts to life only from stored information.

During our earlier years, we are mostly in the slower brainwave states, which is hypnotic, and may pick up the wrong messaging and make it our truth. Primary caregivers that feel unworthy may unconsciously say things to a child that makes them feel unlovable. Primary caregivers that live with depression may neglect a child's emotional needs causing the child to feel undeserving of those needs. Although we eventually develop a stronger mind which increases our willpower, we are still operating most of the time through our belief system which is programmed into the subconscious mind from early childhood.

The imagination of a child is unreserved and expansive due to the undeveloped logical mind and lack of life experiences. The imagination may exaggerate the safety of the child since the childhood mind is only concerned with survival. Any possible threat to one's survival can become overwhelming to the child. A possible threat includes any neglect, knowingly or unknowingly, of the child's emotional or physical needs. The childhood mind would create a belief that they are unworthy of getting their needs met. As fears within the mind continue to feed the child with inflated thoughts of unworthiness, the child begins to expect others to be disappointed in who they are. This creates low self-esteem and a constant need for security. Feelings of unworthiness continue to get suppressed below conscious awareness so the child can gain a sense of safety. This causes the child, without their conscious awareness, to continuously seek the approval of others to ensure continued safety. As time goes on, these buried feelings are forgotten about on a conscious level but continue to affect the life of the child right into their adulthood.

# Chapter 2

## Self-Rejection and the False Self

*"Your purpose is to be yourself. You don't have to run anywhere to become someone else. You are wonderful just as you are"*

*~ Thich Nhat Hanh*

There are many things that happen during childhood that could cause a child to feel unworthy of love. Many children grow up in a very dysfunctional home keeping their mind in constant confusion about their lovability and safety. Some children have grown up in a one parent home, causing them to question why the other parent has abandoned them. Many children are victims of school bullies who crave attention and power. Some children may have a parent that is depressed or ill, drug or alcohol dependent, narcissistic or controlling. There are many reasons a child could feel unworthy and, therefore, unsafe in the world. Unfortunately, these feelings are so intense for a child that the child's mind cannot properly process them. This is known as "emotional trauma." Emotional trauma is caused by any experience that is overwhelming and thereby causes an inability to integrate it fully. It changes a child's life because it affects their ability to feel secure in a big unpredictable world.

Emotional trauma changes us and can leave an indelible mark of shame and unworthiness if we do not address it properly. The longer it lingers, the more we find it difficult to love ourselves. Since emotional traumas are difficult to process as children, the emotions get suppressed into the subconscious mind and live through us our entire lives unless we properly and fully heal them. Trauma causes a disconnect from oneself as a strategy to escape pain. Due to a lack of healthy coping mechanisms and emotional maturity during our younger years, we had no choice but to bury the emotions that overwhelmed us. We have a choice now.

We all know, on an intellectual level, that children are innocent beings that are filled with the desire for love and attention. What we do not understand is that when we encounter adults who seem off-balance in some way, these adults were once the innocent child that had to fight for love and many times to no avail. Due to unfortunate experiences in their childhood or due to an overactive imagination that led to irrational fears, parts of their whole self are trapped in an unresolved fearful past. Since these parts of the whole self are out of conscious awareness, the mature adult mind does not know these parts exists and the effect they have on them now.

When we talk about self-love, we do not realize that below the surface of conscious awareness lie the parts of us that feel rejected, inferior, unacceptable, and unworthy of love. This means we are never fully in that place of self-love. We are only in a place of partial acceptance with an ego mind that denies the existence of any feelings of unworthiness. This is because the ego's biggest fear is rejection of the whole self. Therefore, any feelings of inadequacy must be kept out of conscious awareness.

Keeping our substandard feelings about ourselves outside of our awareness is a protective strategy. The ego mind is protecting the whole-self from being rejected by the world due to there being unacceptable glitches in the whole-self. These glitches are the parts of us that we have not fully accepted as our own. The ego mind sees these glitches as a threat to our safety. The ego mind is more about human survival than it is about the spiritual journey of discovering ourselves. The ego does not want to hurt us. It wants to keep us safe from rejection by the world, so it works hard to keep inferior thoughts and emotions suppressed. This keeps us in conflict because we have not learned how to heal our rejected parts so we can live fully in our spiritual power. Our spiritual power lies within the divine truth that we are all on a journey to self-love and an understanding and appreciation of unity love consciousness. The most important part of this journey is to keep working towards self-love even when others cause us to question our lovability. Working towards self-love means healing and releasing all the emotional traumas that cause us to believe we are not lovable.

If we are attached to the past due to unresolved emotional trauma and we fear our future because we feel betrayed by the past, then we are being pulled away from our spirit and into the mental mind of the ego. The more we are in denial about who we really are, the more we focus on the fabricated false self which keeps us from deep diving into true spirituality. The false self is what our ego has created so that we can be accepted by society. The false self only exhibits the parts of the whole self that we believe are acceptable to the world, together with the personality traits we adopted to meet the expectations of our primary caregivers. This is not self-love – it is survival love.

Living through the false self is a safety comfort left over from childhood. "If I can meet your expectations of me, then you will accept me." This created a pattern where you are now disconnected from your authentic self and solely reliant on your false self to keep you safe in the world. The ego, your protector, becomes your navigator in life, instead of your intuitive senses – your inner truth. True spirituality is going deep into the darkness where we hide aspects of ourselves, not only to see our vulnerabilities and disowned parts, but to discover their innocence and true spiritual essence.

The world we live in is quite challenging, and for some, it is extremely difficult and complicated. From the way we are raised, to the demands of the educational system, the dictates of our culture, societal expectations, financial and health concerns, and the conflicts we encounter in our personal relationships, we are always dealing with emotions. It is these emotions that cause us to decide, consciously or unconsciously, if we are loved and safe in our environment. How can we embody self-love with so many fluctuating emotions that cause us to question our worth and security in the world?

To start our healing process, we must heal the unresolved pain of the past so we can live in the present moment. In the present moment, we can focus on the current challenges without the emotions from the past intensifying them. If we stay emotionally tied to a difficult past that is now and forever gone, then we are going to suffer in the present moment. This will hold us back from loving ourselves and creating a better future. We will keep taking momentous steps forward and then sabotaging steps backwards because we will not have complete focus on our current goals.

To stay on a path towards self-love, it starts with resolving our emotional disharmony. This means healing the parts of us that felt rejected a long time ago. These are the parts of us that are trapped in the past, live in shame, and feel unworthy of love. We do not see the miracle of life that we are. We are still reliant on the approval from the world. This is how we are conditioned to believe we are not enough. How can we suddenly feel worthy enough to navigate this world with confidence, strength and determination if we have memories of feeling disempowered and unworthy? How can we stop relying on the world to evaluate us and just trust that we are one of life's miracles and deserve to be loved even if we didn't feel loved? We must give ourselves permission to release others from the responsibility to make us feel whole. We must know in our hearts that we are already whole, we just don't feel that way because of the emotional traumas that make us feel fragmented. These unhealed parts of us are driving us to seek acceptance from a world that is highly judgmental. We may not realize how affected we are by our past traumas because we are living through our false self that the ego mind claims as worthy, while parts of our true self are trapped in an emotional state of self-rejection.

As we work towards self-acceptance, we must realize that there is nothing wrong with us, but only that it went wrong for us. The same is true for those that caused us to question our value. They are also seeking self-acceptance. Their inability to show us love and support is an indication that they too are in self-denial of who they really are. In our truth, we express divine love and compassion. If we are not receiving this from others, then they are not in their truth. This journey is about understanding human consciousness and the fears that keep us from loving ourselves. Instead, we take the inability of others to show and express love as an indication of our worth. We then created a false version of ourselves that would mold us into their expectations of us so we can gain their acceptance. We then use the same tactics in our adult life because we don't want to feel rejected. The false self becomes who we believe we are while we suffer the slow burn of losing our true selves. This is known as self-abandonment and is a survival strategy that pleases the ego but damages the connection to our true selves.

We cannot continue to deny who we are. We must find a way to allow ourselves to be authentic without the fear of abandonment, rejection, judgment, or condemnation. Unfortunately, our world is filled with so much fear and criticism that it is not easy to stay on the journey to self-love. When we return to self-love, there is no fear of judgment by others. We will know that the judgments of others reflect their feelings of unworthiness. We will live a life of authenticity, non-judgment, and compassion for self and others.

Until we reach that level again, we will fluctuate about who we are and what our value and significance is in this world. In the higher truth, we are rising above the false doctrines, dogmas and beliefs that do not align with love. There are no opinions, judgments, views or beliefs in the higher truth. It just is. It is pure, unadulterated love that permeates all souls. When souls experience this celestial energy within them, they are remembering who they are as light bodies occupying a physical form to experience the material world and learn the truth about authentic love and its ability to renew and revitalize a soul that got trapped in fear. That is how we learn the value of the love we embody and why it is important to be authentic in this challenging world. Although we will experience lessons of nonlove along the physical journey, we will always re-align ourselves with the higher truth when we seek it from the heart.

When we are in our higher truth, the low-level thoughts and opinions of others cannot affect us. We will see these others as not loving themselves, so they cannot express love. We will not take them personally. We will have great love for them, even when they cannot show love for themselves. We will know that they got lost along the journey and abandoned their true selves for the sake of acceptance. When we are in the higher truth, we see the whole picture around human consciousness. We do not play egocentric games, and we do not chase love. We simply embody love.

# Chapter 3

## The Whole Self, Its Parts and Fragmentation

*"Each of us have the same purpose: To be the best and fullest expression of ourselves"*

*~ Ronda Renée*

All parts of us, whether true or false aspects of ourselves, are significant and worthy of discussion and are collectively referred to herein as the "whole self." To describe the whole-self, I am going to use the model and work of Dr. Carl Jung. Dr. Jung was a Swiss psychiatrist and psychoanalyst born in the late 1800s and is well known for his theories on the parts of the whole self that he called the persona, the shadow, the anima/animus, and the Self.

The *persona* is an inflated image of oneself that is projected into the world as one's true self. The persona was created by the ego personality as a protection against rejection by others in the material world. The persona is the mask one wears to display a character of moral and ethical value to meet the expectations of society. This will allow one to be viewed as someone who can make a significant contribution to the world and, therefore, be deemed an asset to humanity.

It is worth noting that the ego is not a bad or negative part of the whole self as many spiritual leaders may imply. It is a necessary part of the human structure and useful when it is in a healthy state. A healthy ego allows us the strength to push ourselves harder when we need to. It allows us to compete against others in a competition. It also allows us to put on a mask in certain situations that require a different aspect of ourselves in society. This does not mean we are acting from a false self. We put on a mask at work when we need to present ourselves as a professional in our field. We put on a mask when we are around certain people because we feel the need to be self-protective in their presence. If we are aware of the different masks we put on in any given situation and we know it's temporary and useful in the moment, then we are masking ourselves in a healthy ego state. When we put on a mask to hide aspects of ourselves that we believe are inferior, unacceptable, and unworthy, then we are denying our true selves for the purpose of receiving external validation. This is not a healthy ego.

The *shadow-self* is the part of the whole-self that is hidden from the world. The shadow-self contains all the parts of ourselves that we believe are flawed, inferior and unworthy of love and, therefore, not valuable enough for the world. These parts of us are suppressed within the deeper parts of the mind and kept out of conscious awareness by the ego. If these shadow parts start to surface into conscious awareness, the ego mind will cause a distraction so it can ignore their call for attention.

The *anima and the animus* are the feminine and masculine parts of the whole self, respectively. The anima is described as the feminine aspect that lives within the human male and the animus is the masculine aspect that lives within the human female. The feminine aspects of oneself would be expressed through creativity, nurturing and unity. The masculine aspects of oneself would be expressed through power, thought and achievement.

Jung believes we all have aspects of feminine and masculine within the whole of who we are. Due to the societal conditioning of our expected roles in the world, we may hide either our feminine or masculine aspects to conform to these expectations. When we don't allow these aspects of ourselves to be expressed in a healthy way, then we are living through a false self.

The *Self* (capitalized to indicate its sacredness) is what Jung described as wholeness. This is when the parts of the whole-self that have been relegated to the shadow-self due to their inferior nature become healed and, therefore, acceptable. This acceptance allows them to be integrated into the whole self. The same is true for the feminine and masculine energies that make up the whole self. Once these hidden parts are integrated into the whole-self as acceptable parts, the person no longer identifies with the inflated ego mind but feels a sense of balance in the parts that make up the whole-self. With integration and acceptance of our self-rejected parts, the false persona is no longer deemed necessary. Jung called this the process of individuation. This is when one has reached its full potential.

The persona is shaped during childhood because of the child's need to conform to the expectations of its caregivers. It is created by a person wearing a mask to cover up the deep feelings of unworthiness that sit below conscious awareness. They use the mask not only to convince others of their worthiness, but also to convince themselves. Once a persona is created, it causes a split-off of the parts of the whole self that do not measure up to parental and societal expectations. This split-off means to place these rejected parts out of conscious awareness. When feminine or masculine traits are denied, it causes a separation of these aspects from the whole self as well. It is only when all parts of the whole-self are integrated as a whole, without a denial or split-off of parts within oneself, will the mask no longer be necessary, except under a person's full awareness of wearing a mask. This is when a person is now living as Self, and not as a magnified version of oneself. This means self-worth is not questioned and the whole self is no longer in a state of disconnection or fragmentation.

Before oneself can reach the wholeness of the Self, there must be unconditional acceptance of the parts that felt rejected by the world. This requires diving into the parts that live below conscious awareness so they can be healed and integrated into the whole self. The reason these parts sit below awareness is because we learned, at an early age, that these parts should not be seen or expressed because they could lead to rejection and possible abandonment. It is believed by the immature child mind that these occurrences will lead to one's demise. Many of these fears are formed during birth or in the womb.

As young children, we begin to establish various parts of ourselves which then create different aspects of our personality. The aspects of the personality that the child believes are acceptable by their caregivers become a safety net for the child. The aspects of the personality that the child perceives as rejected, denounced, or condemned by the caregivers in their life become suppressed into the shadow self. This is how the child meets the expectations of the world and, therefore, establishes a sense of belonging and safety. As the child matures, the ego becomes more prominent. The ego personality builds strength and tenacity which then forms the persona. The ego builds up the persona and creates a boosted false self to compensate for what the ego believes is deficient in the whole self. This is where we lose our true selves and live through our fragmented self, unknowingly seeking out our missing parts through spiritual practices and superficial connections with others.

Parts of the whole self are formed whenever we need to separate from the whole self. A child with a tendency to be loud may be told by a parent that they are too loud, and it is annoying to the rest of the family. For the child to avoid rejection by the family, the child becomes quiet and reserved. The aspect of the whole self that is loud becomes pushed into the shadow self as a rejected part. When the child becomes an adult, they may find themselves drawn to loud people. Although they get drawn to them, they may complain relentlessly about how annoying their loudness is. This is because they are rejecting their shadow aspect that showed up in another person while at the same time unknowingly seeking connection to their rejected parts.

Another example of separation or fragmentation from the whole self is when a younger version of the whole self has the debilitating experience of grief but does not know how to express it and heal it. This lack of expression causes the grieving part of the whole self to be suppressed below conscious awareness, causing deep sadness throughout one's life. This causes the whole self to seek out someone who is trapped in sadness, but then judges the sadness. They are denying a part within themselves which causes them to reject it in another, while they seek to embody it through another person. They are unknowing seeking out their lost parts. This is what one may call the "mirroring effect." This is when we see parts of ourselves in another person. The idea is for us to recognize the mirror and start working on these hidden aspects of ourselves so they can be integrated back into the whole self. Due to our strong egos and established personas, we fail to see the mirror that has been placed before us.

Parts of the whole self seem to be categorized as either valuable parts or unwanted parts. If we can only love what we believe are familiarly or socially acceptable parts of us, then we have forgotten our true value. We seem to have steered too far away from the spirit of who we are as we rely more on ego to keep us in our protective false personalities. Although in our higher truth, we are perfect divine beings, in this challenging world we feel flawed and many times unsafe. This is because much of the world has been sucked into their ego-selves to assure self-protection, thereby creating personas that are self-serving and many times avoidant of intimate emotions and true divine connections.

During our growing up years, we have observed and examined the influential adults in our environment. If we could match them, then we must be accepted by them. If we could adapt to their expectations of us, then we will not be abandoned by them. If you could imagine what a child mind is experiencing as they continuously seek love, acceptance and belonging as a safety measure, but frequently experience feelings of rejection, then you will understand why so many people feel disconnected and unsafe in the world. The child's mind is very imaginative and what is imagined becomes the reality for the child. If a child perceives that they have been rejected by a caregiver who expressed disappointment in the child, shamed the child in some way, ignored them, or harshly criticized them, the child mind will immediately get trapped in fear thoughts and the associated emotions will get pushed down into the body. These thoughts and emotions are now trapped within the child and will play out through their entire life and affect the way they sees themselves and the world. This causes the child's mind within the adult body to seek out approval from the world, and hence, the fictitious persona. The child's mind is living in fear, while the ego personality blocks access to the associated suppressed emotions and continuously strengthens the persona.

Other ways that children adapt to the expectations of their caregivers is by forming patterns of behavior that they believe will help them connect better with the people they need. Some of these patterns are holding back anger and frustration, remaining quiet and unseen when caregivers are neglectful, not asking for anything that may cause an unwanted reaction and being compliant even when it feels uncomfortable. These are all survival tactics that become part of the false personality. These childhood patterns could play out in one's adult life as people pleasing, not able to set boundaries, unable to express emotions and not expecting anything from anyone. This is the protective ego doing its job to ensure acceptance by the world, and hence the false self.

This disconnect to our true selves is common in our world because so much emphasis is placed on being accepted by society. We are constantly avoiding the pain from the past as the unhealed child parts of us scream for feelings of safety and belonging. Instead, we fluff up our egos and chase love, connection, praise, and validation – the things we needed most in our childhood. This has caused a world of mental mind traps, closed hearts, strong personas, and lots of ego tripping. This has been a generational issue and remains strong today because most people are afraid to release the patterns that kept them safe as a child. The ego has taken over the truth of who we are, keeping us stuck in our fabricated selves while we dim down our light, suppress our inner child and fight for survival in a world that seems quite threatening at times. If we do not come back to our truth, then we will contribute to the generational fragmentation that keeps this world in a state of emotional disconnect. This is the main reason there is a lack of love in the world. The inner war that many are experiencing is being played out in the world on a collective basis. We don't see people as hurt, we see them as controlling, narcissistic, too shy, too brazen, too ignorant, too sensitive, too much or too little. We do not see their inner spirit because it was crushed a long time ago. These are the people that have a challenging time loving themselves. It is not their fault. They are simply unaware of their survival patterns. The people in the world that seem to care about no one except themselves and are outright cruel to others are so disconnected from love, their spirit and life that they find it pleasing to see others suffer. This is not the rule, but the exception, when it comes to the human condition. Most people are seeking connection from a heart space, but live in deep fear of rejection, criticism and nonlove.

No matter how broken we may feel at any given time, we are always whole in our divine truth. It is only when we get caught in the trap of negative thoughts about ourselves that we must pretend to love who we are. So much of our true selves is hidden below our conscious awareness as our false selves show up as well-adjusted human beings. We do not realize that we are longing for our authentic selves underneath our facades of self-acceptance are painful feelings of fragmentation.

The masculine rejects his nurturing-self because he has been conditioned to believe it is a weakness of the masculine. The feminine rejects her power because it may detract from her beauty. This means we are only loving what we have been conditioned to believe are significant and acceptable aspects of ourselves.

Although it is necessary to express our true selves, including our hidden parts, it is important to express ourselves from a healthy mental attitude. If we bring forth our hidden parts and express them in a victimized, self-pity, angry or resentful manner, then we are not expressing from an authentic place, only from the fears of unworthiness. Expression of our true selves comes from the healing and full integration of these hidden parts so we can express ourselves from the divine love we embody. This allows us to forgive ourselves for getting lost in the pain of rejection and forgive others for their inability to live from their authentic selves.

It takes deep internal healing for us to see all humans as divine aspects of the All-Loving Creator that unfortunately got trapped in the emotional challenges of our human experiences. We need to understand, on a higher level, that these challenges have caused many people to live in survival mode and, unfortunately, separated them from their authentic selves.

We may have experienced the adults in our lives acting out through their wounded inner child, but we did not know this as children. Do not hold this against them. They are living through a falsely created self. Much of their true self is suppressed and they are living in a state of disconnect, confusion and painful fragmentation. They are not aware of the fears that are controlling them. They are trying to survive as the memories in their subconscious mind keep telling them that they are deeply flawed. Your compassion towards them is necessary for your own healing. By being compassionate, you are expressing your true divine self in a situation that needs love and compassionate understanding. This means you did not get drawn into their egocentric bubble, but instead stayed in your true essential-self – an aspect of the All-Loving Creator. Be the person you needed them to be for you. This is the only way to keep yourself energetically free from their emotional control over you. If you engage with them on a fear level, then you are letting yourself get entwined with their fear energy. If you show them love because you see their innocence under their false mask, you are expressing compassion towards the hurt child in them and love towards their true divine self. If you forget who you really are, which is a being of love and light, then you jeopardize your inner power and fall into the same egoic trap with them.

All parts of us are longing for feelings of love, worthiness and, above all, safety. The way we seek out safety will be different for all parts because it is based on the unmet needs that caused the split-off from the whole self. Each individual part is trying to get their childhood needs met through their adult relationships, but this is done unconsciously and sometimes in childlike desperate ways. This is why compassion for yourself and for others is important during your self-love journey. Self-love is not something we work towards but a truth we embody once we release the obstacles that keep us from living as our authentic selves.

It seems we are complicated beings and there is a lot to balance. This is true, but it does not mean we should give up. What is important is that we express ourselves from a genuine place. We must find a way to accept, honor and love our authentic selves, even though parts of our authentic selves do not resonate with others. Our true divine selves come from the spirit of love and compassion. In our authentic selves, we do not intentionally cause harm to ourselves or others. We live in a place of cooperation, where we know how to work together for the greater good of all. We came from divine unity and must not let our human experiences take that from us. We must learn how to come back to self-love.

When we are in our false selves due to fragmentation, we are living from a survival place which causes us to be self-serving. Even if we are people pleasing, we are being self-serving. This is because the true motive is to gain acceptance, even if we must give more of ourselves to get that acceptance. By healing what needs to be healed and returning to balance, feelings of wholeness and self-love, we come back to Self. We do not overextend ourselves for acceptance, but we live and share from a place of divine love.

All parts of the whole self must work together for a harmonious life. We are not getting rid of our egos. Our ego mind is part of our third-dimensional reality, and it is a part of the human experience. If we stop denying parts of ourselves, then we can balance the ego mind, so it does not have so much power over us. When we give our power to the ego to protect ourselves from rejection, we are creating the split between the ego mind and the true divine self. This is not conducive to living a whole and balanced life.

The fragmentation that we experience due to splitting off parts of ourselves is meant to teach us the valuable lesson of self-love. We are not loving ourselves if we are rejecting ourselves. Fragmentation causes extreme distress in the whole self. It is that distress that is teaching us how to rise above the illusions of unworthiness and come back to our divine truth.

As humans, we will always be challenged, but it is how we meet those challenges that will be the deciding factor of our ability to lead ourselves back to divine truth. Every time we heal a piece of us, we are closer to experiencing self-love.

# Chapter 4

## The Emotional Needs of Humanity

*"When we heal ourselves, others are healed. When we nurture our dreams, we give birth to the dreams of humankind. When we walk as loving aspects of the Earth Mother, we become the fertile, life-giving Mothers of the Creative Force. When we honor our bodies, our health, and our emotional needs, we make space for our dreams to come into being. When we speak the truth from our healed hearts, we allow life abundant to continue on our Mother Planet"*

*~ Jamie Sams*

Before we can understand how we unknowingly form different parts of ourselves, it is important to understand how the childhood mind functions. The childhood mind does not understand logic and does not spend time analyzing situations. What the childhood mind does do is watch, listen, and learn from others. The child's mind is mostly concerned with the safety of themselves and for those they need and love. A child feels safe when there is peace in their environment and their needs are being met. Most children get their physical needs met, but most children do not get their emotional needs met. This is due to their caregivers not being aware of the emotional needs of children. These caregivers were most likely raised with a focus on their physical needs and, therefore, were lacking in their own emotional needs. There seems to be an ancestral trap of emotional deficiencies that has plagued many generations due to too much focus on physical survival. We can change this course by learning the reason we are here and working towards bringing more love into the world. We need to understand the importance of meeting our emotional needs and the consequences of ignoring what they are. When our emotional needs are not met, we do not love ourselves and we do not feel safe in the world.

The emotional needs of a child include feeling unconditional love, receiving empathy, getting validation, having the ability to set boundaries, being accepted by their caregivers, being heard, having a sense of belonging and feeling significant. Let me unpack each of these for a greater understanding of their importance.

*Unconditional Love* is without conditions. If a primary caregiver makes the child feel that their love for them is conditioned upon them meeting certain expectations of the caregiver, then the child's need for unconditional love is not met. When a caregiver places expectations upon a child and the child for some reason is unable to meet those expectations and this disappoints the caregiver, the child will feel that they are a failure and, therefore, not deserving of love. This will cause the child to feel unworthy of love in all their relationships, right into their adulthood, unless they can meet the expectations of the people for which they seek love from. This can cause a part of the child's mind to suppress their own needs so they can meet the needs of others to receive love. The part of them that feels like a failure becomes suppressed into the shadow self and lives in fear of disappointing others. The ego mind then creates a false self (persona) that does not disappoint anyone. For survival purposes, the child may become a people pleaser.

It is important to note that the child's mind is very imaginative and could wrongly perceive that the caregiver is disappointed in them. A caregiver may want to see their child succeed in something and may even push them towards success, but this could cause an irrational fear in the child's mind that if they fail, they will be deemed a disappointment. This could cause stress in the child's body and create fears of unworthiness into their adult life.

Many caregivers hold back love and affection as a punishment for the child who is not behaving to the expectations of the caregiver. This is usually a behavior that the caregiver learned from their caregivers when they were growing up. The child may go to great lengths to earn back love and affection because they believe they cannot survive without it. As an adult, they may feel they have to work extra hard to earn someone's love and affection. This will keep them under constant emotional stress which can then lead to other problems.

*Empathy* is the ability to understand the feelings of another. If a primary caregiver insinuates or tells a child that they should not feel a certain way or that their feelings are foolish or unnecessary, then the childhood emotional need is not met. The child feels that no one understands them. Sometimes the caregiver cannot empathize with the feelings of the child because they believe there is an exaggeration of feelings, or the feelings are completely imagined. It is not uncommon for caregivers to dismiss a child's feelings because they do not know how to support them, most likely because they did not receive support when they were children. Sometimes, the caregiver rejects what the child feels because the child was able to shake up some feelings within the shadow part of the caregiver, causing them to reject the child's feelings, just like they rejected these feelings within themselves.

If a child falls and skins their knee, they may seek sympathy from a caregiver. If the caregiver tells them to brush it off and continue to play outside, the child may feel that no one cares about them when they get hurt. This could show up later in life as someone who never complains or asks for help when they are not feeling well to avoid the pain of rejection.

It is normal for children to get frustrated at times because there is so much that they do not understand. If they express their frustration, it may be met with disapproval, criticism and maybe scolding. When the need for empathy is not met, it causes the child to relegate to the shadow self the part of them that seeks understanding, empathy, or sympathy for what they are experiencing. As they grow up, they start living more through the persona that they do not need anyone's empathy or sympathy and may even unconsciously and automatically reject the genuine concern of another.

*Validation* is affirming the feelings and emotions of another as true, real, valid, and worth being recognized. When a primary caregiver shuts down the feelings or emotions of a child, they are giving the child the impression that their feelings and emotions are not valid, or they do not matter. This could cause the child to shut down their feelings and emotions to avoid further rejection. The child suppresses into the shadow self the part of them that needs to express how they feel. As an adult, they keep their feelings and emotions to themselves because they believe they are not worthy of being heard or they fear ridicule or rejection of their expressed emotions. They are unable to label their own emotions because they keep questioning their own feelings. They will vacillate between different feelings because they cannot find a way to validate what they truly feel. The child grows into an adult with a persona of someone who is in full control of their feelings. The adult self may exhibit an unemotional, stern, or insensitive demeaner. The part of the whole self that is suppressed is deemed by the ego mind to be an overly emotional, overly sensitive and a pathetic part of the whole self and, therefore, must be rejected.

*Boundaries* allows you to be in touch with your emotional needs and allows you to honor them. This means saying no to things that do not align with your values or needs. It is respecting your personal time and space when needed without worrying about the expectations of others. When a child's boundaries are not respected, they may believe that they are not entitled to have boundaries. This could show up in adulthood as allowing others to take advantage of them because they are afraid to set a boundary. The ego mind wants to avoid rejection, so it labels any people pleasing tendencies as one who is selfless and will always give their time when needed. What is not known is that there is another part of the whole self that wants their personal time respected but hides this part of themselves to avoid rejection.

*Acceptance* means being accepted for who you are no matter how many mistakes you make in the process of learning about yourself, others, and the world you live in. Acceptance of who you are is a childhood need that is rarely met due to the inability of others to accept themselves as good enough for the world. When a primary caregiver criticizes, judges, or condemns a child, the child feels they are not acceptable as they are. They create a strong belief that they must change and adapt to the adults' expectations of them, or they will get rejected and possibly abandoned.

Many times, the adult projects onto the child their own shadow parts, causing the child to suppress the same needs that the adult suppressed. When someone projects their hidden emotions onto another, it means that they are expressing a part of them that they are not consciously aware of. Projection onto others is a way to express unacknowledged negative emotions about oneself, while allowing oneself to believe that these emotions belong to the other person. This is done unconsciously and can cause severe psychological suffering for a child.

If a child seeks to get a childhood need met that their primary caregiver was unable to receive from their caregivers, it could cause the adult to vehemently reject it for the child. This is because the caregiver had rejected it within themselves during their childhood. They are not purposely rejecting the need of the child;

they are rejecting their own shadow part through the child. If they cannot accept it in themselves, then they cannot accept it in another. By the caregiver's rejection of the child's need for acceptance, the child now suppresses this need. This part will stay hidden while the false self takes over the personality and causes the whole self to strive for acceptance through other means. These other means include financial stability, a high-level career, attractive physical appearance, or material status. None of these things will bring the whole self to a feeling of balance and wholeness because they are not coming from the true self. The suppressed parts will continue to be split-off and create fragmentation. As this part continues to stay in the shadow self, the persona exhibits someone who feels confident and balanced, while there is a part of them that feels inferior.

*Being Heard* is another childhood need that is rarely met. Sadly, so many brilliant minds are being wasted. When a child is speaking and their voice is often ignored or the child cannot maintain the attention of others, they form a belief that their voice, opinions, ideas, or personal input on matters are not important and not worth expressing. If a child is angry, frustrated or has an outburst of emotion, the child is trying to be heard. When the primary caregiver does not take the time to help the child work through the emotional crisis, but instead scolds the child for their outburst, the child may shut down any intense emotions that need expression. The child then becomes the unemotional adult which is the false self and categorized by others as the cold-hearted and distant person.

Many adults that have great knowledge that would be beneficial to others do not share this gift because they suppress the part of them that feels unworthy of being heard. They may get frustrated at the inability to speak up and share their wisdom. This is a denial of one's true self and, therefore, its suppression denies self-love.

*Belonging* means being and feeling accepted by our familial tribe, expanded community and the world. One of our biggest fears is being alone and not cared for by others. When we feel like we belong where we are, we feel secure and valuable.

Tribal consciousness is part of our generational cellular memory. We thrive when we feel the support of others around us. Without that support and a feeling of belonging, we could become adults who live in fears of loneliness and abandonment. These fears will cause the birth of the false self and allow for the creation of a persona that joins every group, becomes agreeable to the group members, and adapts to their expectations, all to ensure their safety in the world. Being tossed from the tribe means non-survival. This is the reason the false self had to be formed. It will ensure that the whole self does not end up alone.

*Significance* ties in with our sense of value in the world. We cannot feel significant if we feel unheard, undervalued, unappreciated or unloved. We can only feel significant if we are good enough to contribute something to the world. If we do not believe we can, then we can feel a sense of despair and self-disappointment. If we feel insignificant, we do not feel like we belong in the world. This can lead to deep depression as oneself battles with their inner fears of worthlessness. Since feeling significant is a childhood need, a lack of it will cause the adult self to seek some form of significance and, therefore, obtain a sense of value. This is done through the material world where ego is prominent, rather than the internal world of self-love. The false self becomes the driving force in life and the authentic self remains hidden.

The authentic you is aware of your worth regardless of life experiences. The ego self focuses on ways of obtaining feelings of safety, a sense of belonging and significance, while subconscious fears of unworthiness continue to haunt the mind. The ego mind can create distractions when feelings of unworthiness try to mess with our fake feelings of significance, but that is only because it wants us to feel valued and safe. The ego must reject any parts of the whole self that do not align with society's definition of significance. If you did not feel significant as a child, chances are you struggle with self-love.

Now that I have broken down each childhood need, let us now look at the bigger picture. I want to start with that none of what I am discussing in this book is about parent bashing or negative thoughts towards those that lack the emotional maturity to see our divine worth due to their dysfunctional upbringing. Most people are trapped in survival consciousness, so they are not exhibiting their true selves. What you do not like about them is their false self that was created by the ego mind for safety. There needs to be a higher understanding of human consciousness to release ourselves from their ego trap. This ego trap is a generational issue and one that needs deep repair. Being our true selves is the only way we can transcend this continuous cycle of unworthiness.

As you read through this book, always remember that the child's mind is pure imagination. There is no analytic, logical, or theoretical consciousness – only a need for safety. The perceptions of a child's mind are not the same as the matured adult mind. The impressions within the child's mind can be completely distorted from the facts. The difficult part is that these childhood impressions, whether real or imagined, become the truth within the lower levels of consciousness that will influence the conscious mind as the child grows up.

We are and always will be whole as divine beings created from the highest octave of love. Human experiences that caused us to question our value in this world have created split-off versions of ourselves which now keep us in internal conflict. It is only in our minds that this split occurs. It is created by false narratives of who we are and then causes the protective energy of the ego mind to step in and take control over our true divine selves. This is to avoid the feeling of the split. We may feel the disconnect, but we do not know what is happening - we only know that we feel unbalanced and not whole. This causes us to seek wholeness in the material world. We unknowingly formed false parts of ourselves to compensate for those missing parts. This was done as a survival strategy and that is why it is so hard to undo these fabricated personality traits. They are considered our survival source. Why would we want to return to our authentic selves when we believe our authentic selves have been rejected? To avoid further rejection, we must keep up the façade. We are focused on what the world expects of us, as we deny our true lovable and valuable selves. We found our value in our false selves because our false selves were better received by the world. Although this is a strong protective energy to carry within us, we are not balanced, nor do we feel whole. We feel fragmented because we do not acknowledge the genuine parts of us that became split from our awareness.

Since we do not love these parts of ourselves and we continue to reject them, then we are not loving who we are. We love who we pretend to be. The important thing to remember is that this is not done on purpose. We are not trying to deceive the world or ourselves – we are simply ensuring our survival. This means we learned to adapt to the environment that we believe can keep us safe. We forgot that we are infinite beings of light that can never be broken or destroyed. This does not mean we should jump in front of a moving train to prove we can never die; it only means that we have the power of the divine within us and that our true selves cannot be negated because of the fears and insecurities we accumulated over time.

Whether we are still in our human birth suit or have left our physical bodies, we are and always will be perfect divine beings created from divine love. As we grow and learn on our physical journeys, the challenges become less, and the embodiment of self-love becomes stronger. The hard part is getting through the emotional challenges that cause us to question our worth in this judgmental world.

We do not need to fix ourselves. We just need to rise above the lower-level consciousness of survival. We do not need to pretend to feel worthy. We need to see our value through the eyes of our Creator. Being authentic means transcending into the divine truth and leaving behind the fabricated tales of abandonment, rejection, guilt, shame, and unworthiness that took over our innocent souls. This can only keep us stuck in life, living through a rigid persona, and continuously seeking our lost parts through others. This is unintentional self-deception, and we need to return to our inner light and see our innocence within the behavioral patterns that were meant to save us, not harm us. We must relearn our true values so we can come back to who we really are. If we are genuinely confident in who we are, there is no force on this planet that can cause us to reject ourselves.

All parts of us that were suppressed into the shadow self are not experiencing love – only fear. This means no matter how hard we try to get our childhood needs met in our adult lives, we will always feel fragmented. If we do not love all parts of ourselves, then we are creating barriers to authentic self-love. All parts of us deserve recognition, love, and unconditional acceptance. We must be the ones to provide these emotional needs to ourselves because those we relied on were not capable of meeting our needs. We are no longer children, so we no longer need to rely on others for our survival. What we need now is to come back to our authentic selves that we unknowingly disconnected from as children.

The versions of the whole self still stuck in the emotional crisis are still hiding, stuck in fears of rejection and afraid to be seen or heard. They have not been integrated into the rest of the whole self so they are not able to experience growing up. Our ego minds see them as weak, useless, inferior, unlovable, and unworthy aspects of the whole self and, therefore, must be annihilated. Although we cannot kill off these parts, the ego mind can create a barrier to them so that we do not realize their existence within us. Since we cannot love these parts, we must make sure they stay out of our awareness, so we believe they are non-existent. This makes us feel superficially whole, while we also feel fragmented.

The ability to receive acceptance and approval is always within the whole-self. It is not until we authentically love who we are that we will stop seeking acceptance and approval outside of ourselves. Unfortunately, we will never get approval outside of us because we are seeking it from a world that is also trapped in their ego minds. They cannot give us what they cannot give to themselves. Life becomes a big game of ego chess and it's not what our Creator meant for us. We were sent here to learn the value of love.

Until we learn the real reason we came to this planet, we will remain stuck in an energetic trap of fear that continues to move through generations, keeping the collective human consciousness in a constant stream of survival energies. As children, we absorbed this energy which feels like a trap because it is a trap. As adults, we must learn how to release ourselves from this trap and seek the higher truth – that we are miraculous beings of light and fear is an illusion of the mental mind. Everything is within the levels of the mind, which need to be fully explored for real change to take place. Once we clear the distorted reality that is playing out from the lower levels of the mind, we will seek the higher truth and release our minds from misconceptions, deceptions, and confusion about who we are as human and spirit.

# Chapter 5

## The Soul's Vibration and the Physical Body

*"If you want to find the secrets of the universe, think in terms of energy, frequency and vibration"*

*~ Nikola Tesla*

When we think of the soul of who we are, we may think of it as our energy body. All energy carries its own vibration. Emotions are energy so they carry their own vibration. The speed at which an emotion vibrates is its frequency. You may have heard people say that their vibration is low or that they are vibing high. The emotions we are experiencing, including the emotions that are buried deep within the soul, all have their own frequency and collectively are affecting the way our energy body vibrates. If we are feeling sad because we are hurt from a break-up, then our soul's vibration will be low, lethargic, and lackluster because the frequency of sadness is slow and sluggish. If we are happy because our employer gave us a good review with a raise, it would increase our vibration to a higher frequency because we are feeling valued, inspired, motivated, and determined. Our emotions will fluctuate from time to time, but the more we vibrate at a higher frequency, the better we are going to feel.

As human beings with souls vibrating to certain frequencies based on our emotional state, we may be stuck in a lower vibration due to low-level emotions that are lingering in our soul. Every time these emotions are triggered by a new emotional situation, we strengthen the energy of these low-level emotions. When we give them more energetic power, we may be giving them control over our higher-level emotions. Our unresolved emotional patterns from the past prevent us from holding onto good feelings about our earthly journey. With every new situation that causes us to feel bad, our energy body immediately shifts to a heavier feeling because there is already a vibrational match for it within the body. Every current negative emotion will intensify the ones that are still unresolved. These triggers will not stop until we heal the pain of the past.

Light emotions are joy, happiness, love, connection, and peace. The heavier emotions are sadness, anger, guilt, shame, resentment, and hate. As we experience these different emotions, our energy bodies experience a shift in vibration. The frequencies that will be the strongest are the frequencies that are constant in our energy body. If we do not have an emotional past that needs healing, then we will not feel overwhelmed by current situations because there would be no lower energy pocket to hook into. It would be easier to work through a current emotional challenge that needs positive attention. We will be able to find a creative solution to the matter because our energy body is in a healthy vibration.

Your soul is the divine essence of who you are, but the soul plays a bigger role than you may realize. Your soul is not only the spiritual aspect of your whole self, but also the life force behind the way you navigate the physical journey. How your soul vibrates determines how your reality will unfold for you. This is because our major life decisions are determined by the thoughts, feelings, and emotions that we are experiencing at any given time. If we fake being happy, but are internally sad and depressed, then our vibration will be low. We will not see much progress in our lives even though we may appear to be happy and ambitious. We may strive for more but find ourselves unconsciously holding back. This is because we are reaching our safety limit. Going beyond this would be a risk for rejection. We are experiencing mental confusion as to why we are not moving forward, as our physical bodies feel sluggish and stagnant. Since all levels of our consciousness are entangled within each other, one will affect the other simultaneously. When the physical body feels heavy and unmotivated, chances are the mental mind is experiencing low-level thoughts and the associated emotions held in the body are weighing it down. The only way to begin balancing out these energies is to work with the thoughts and emotions that keep us stuck instead of fighting off triggers and running towards spiritual healing for a quick fix. It is our birthright to be at peace with who we are, but first we must heal and integrate the parts of ourselves that are contained within these lower vibrational energies.

The word "soul" has varying definitions but is most referred to as an immortal part of the whole self. It is immortal because it is made of energy and energy cannot die but can only change its form. Part of the physical body is the brain. Many people think of the brain as the mind. The brain is a physical structure, while the mind is more like a body of energy because it is consciousness. Some scholars refer to the brain as a receiver of consciousness, like an antenna.

Consciousness refers to individual awareness of oneself and its environment. This includes awareness of one's unique thoughts, feelings, emotions, sensations, memories, and perceptions. Low-level consciousness from unhealed emotional trauma keeps the mind from being highly aware of its current environment. This is because too much of our energy is stuck in unresolved painful memories. When we heal and integrate these unhealed parts of ourselves, we become more aware, have more clarity of mind, and feel more in control of our lives. Otherwise, we live in a fragmented body of consciousness, which then creates a distorted reality.

All our emotions, which are born from our thoughts, feelings and perceptions about ourselves, others, and our environment, are sending information through the body by the vibrational energy they carry. This energy is then interpreted by the body as a good, bad, or indifferent messaging. If the message is interpreted as bad because it's in a lower vibration, then it signals the nervous system to respond to an incoming threat. Whenever the energy of an emotional situation in current time matches stored lower vibrational energy, the nervous system will be triggered by what feels like a threat. Whenever the nervous system is triggered, it will cause a fight, flight, or freeze survival response. This causes the body to release stress chemicals, like adrenaline and cortisol. If this happens often due to growing up in a dysfunctional family, being in an unhealthy relationship, staying at a stressful job, living with a serious illness or any other low vibrational situation, the body will be continuously releasing these stress chemicals. Eventually, the body becomes addicted to this flow of chemicals, which causes the person to unconsciously seek out low vibrational situations. Although the mind may be trying to get to a place of peace, the body is craving the familiar adrenaline flow that becomes activated by negative situations.

Since we are not aware that we may be carrying low frequency emotions from our childhood, our bodies could have been slowly releasing these stress chemicals over the years. This could cause low energy, adrenal fatigue, lack of desire, and a general sense of malaise. When we encounter drama in our lives, we suddenly get a big adrenaline rush which gives us back our energy, but only temporarily. Eventually, the low energy returns, and the body begins to crave another adrenaline rush.

When our souls are in a low vibration for a lengthy period, we are depleting our energy source and seeking energy reserves outside of ourselves for that pick me up. Although it may seem like we have energy to spare because we are so busy with our lives, eventually our physical bodies will force a shutdown to hold onto whatever energy it can salvage. This is not only because these emotions are still active, but also because our ego minds are constantly monitoring them to ensure they do not get revealed. We are using up energy resources when it is not necessary. It is more important to expend our energy towards personal growth, rather than fighting against suppressed emotions.

Every time we go into a survival response, we use up our energy. It can be exhausting to the physical body and the soul.

When we are always in survival response, it is hard to love ourselves. We are too focused on staying safe, rather than learning from our experiences and gaining higher wisdom. As part of learning to love ourselves again, we must consider how not loving ourselves affects our mental minds, our physical bodies, our soul bodies, and our energy resources. Unstable emotions mean unstable energy body. Unstable energy body means exhaustion in all levels of our being right down to the physical level. This is not working towards self-love. It is a form of self-sabotage, although unknowingly.

One of the lowest vibrating emotions is shame. When someone feels a deep sense of shame, it is difficult for them to see any good in themselves. The feeling of shame makes you want to just sink down into the earth and disappear. It could even show up in the physical body with the head held down to avoid looking up into the world – a fear of being noticed. People holding onto shame believe they are bad and on an unconscious level may sabotage anything good that comes into their lives. This is a form of self-punishment that is done by the part of the whole self that sits in those relentless feelings of disgrace and despair. The adult mental mind might resort to alcohol, recreational drugs, or other mind-altering substances to block out these overwhelming feelings while the energy body becomes depleted of its vital energy resources.

People can get trapped in the pain of shame when they are young children and such low frequency feelings can run quite deep. As these children grow into adults, they may show bouts of depression and anger. People will label them as a hot mess, crazy, bizarre, and even a waste to society. This is unfair because the power shame can have over the consciousness of the whole self is extremely strong and quite debilitating for anyone experiencing it. It will take some deep healing for someone living in shame to pull themselves back to their divine truth. When society continues to shame them for how they show up in life, then the pain of their shame just continues to deepen.

How many times does a child need to hear "you should be ashamed of yourself" before they start to believe it? How can a child who lives in severe poverty not feel ashamed? The school kid that gets teased for being overweight cannot help but feel ashamed. Along with feelings of shame are feelings of embarrassment and fear.

Notice that all these internal feelings of shame come from something experienced in the environment. We have so much reliance on our environment to show us who we are, and this is why so many people are emotionally stagnant. The person experiencing shame does not realize that anything outside of them has nothing to do with who they are. They will spend years in misery, most likely in therapy, and probably living a very unhealthy lifestyle. The part of them that is feeling ashamed is so low in their vibration that it can take the whole self down.

Another low frequency emotion is guilt. Guilt is when someone feels that they did something bad. Guilt can make us self-punish, lose sleep, and fear we will be taken down by some higher power. Feeling guilty can happen anytime in our lives, but when it happens as children, we tend to feel it more. This is because we feel so vulnerable. If we feel we cannot protect ourselves and we believe we deserve to be punished, we will assume punishment is imminent. This causes us to feel very anxious as the energy of guilt can bring us to our knees as we beg for forgiveness. We are always waiting for the penalty. This blocks us from striving for goodness in our lives. We must first repent before we can receive the gift of happiness. Feeling guilty is not a bad thing. It means we have a conscience. We believe we committed a wrong as the frequency of guilt pulls on the energy body. It is not easy to shake these heavy feelings unless we can authentically forgive ourselves.

Sometimes, we are made to feel guilty by others because they were projecting their guilt onto us. Once we hold the emotion of guilt, we have a challenging time letting it go. We just go on with our lives while there is a part of us that wants to destroy us for being a bad person. The quality of life is low because we do not believe we deserve the good. We unconsciously keep pulling in the bad to keep us in that self-punishing mode.

These emotions are living through parts of the whole self, but their heaviness is felt by the whole self. What the whole self is feeling is the energy drain and the need for internal balance.

Not only does not loving the whole self cause us to feel emotionally drained, it can also have devasting effects on the physical body. This is because when our energy becomes depleted, our immune system must fight harder. Eventually the immune system gets broken down from exhaustion. There is plenty of evidence showing the connection between unhealthy emotions and physical illness. When we have a challenging time releasing low frequency emotions, and then we use up our energy fighting off emotional triggers, we our putting our physical bodies under immense stress. This underlying stress is not easily recognizable. It gradually drains our energy reserves as we strive for a better life. What we do not understand is that this energy decline may eventually lead to physical issues. The only way to replenish our energy reserves is to raise the vibration of our energy bodies. We need to do the inner work that will bring a peaceful resolution to the memories that are still actively seeking our attention. Every trigger is a message that something is unsettled within the consciousness of the whole self. We need to stop ignoring the messages. Many of these messages are speaking through the complaints we make about the ills of our physical bodies.

When low-level emotions are outside of awareness because they are stuck in the shadow self, we tend to believe our discomfort is strictly physical. We must look at the whole self when we do our healing work. This means the mental mind, the shadow self, the physical self, the emotional state, and the energy body. We must be in tune with all these parts, bring them into balance and keep moving forward on our self-love journey.

Our souls are always seeking a vibrational match. We start to align with the people that we are surrounded by. This begins at the first stages of life when we felt the need to adapt to our environment for survival purposes. If we do not adapt, then we do not know where we belong in the world. This is where we begin to lose contact with our spirit. We have many bouts of confusion going on in our mental mind as we grow and learn about ourselves and the world. We have desires that get suppressed, we have feelings that are ignored, we have rules that are hard to follow, and we have demands placed upon us that we cannot always adhere to. This keeps us on constant high alert in our mental mind and our vibration low in the energy body. We are always trying to find that safe place. On an unconscious level, we are still doing this. This keeps us vibrating at the lower level most of the time. Healing low frequency emotions is the key to coming back to our true selves and a well-balanced energy body.

Our souls long for peace. If we keep fluctuating in our emotions due to unresolved emotional trauma, we spoil the soul's desire for life. This can bring us into a deep depression, which means the soul needs a rest from all the difficulties. We cannot keep pampering the physical body and chasing spiritual practices to constantly re-energize the soul. We need to go deeper into the soul and find out why we need a constant shift back into inner peace. We are always seeking to fill up our energy reserves, but we must find out why we keep getting drained. If low frequency emotions are using up our energy, then we are just Band-Aiding the issue by depending on spiritual remedies outside of ourselves. It is important for our soul's evolution that we revisit these unhealed emotions and give them the love and attention they deserve. This will stop the constant wavering of emotions and will help keep our energy flow moving effortlessly, harmoniously, and consistently.

We have more control over our energy reserves than we realize. We need to stop being afraid of the pain we experienced in the past. Whatever we experienced is not an indication of our worth. We must remember that we are emotional human beings that just want to be at peace, feel safe and live in the vibration of love. It takes some work on our part to get there. We must realize that we are worth the time and effort it takes to work our way back to self-love.

There is a divine purpose for everything our souls experience during our physical journey. Let us not dwell on what should have been and focus on what could be as we learn more about who we truly are.

# Chapter 6

## The Purpose of the Shadow
## Self and the False self

*"To confront a person with his shadow is to show him his own light. Once one has experienced a few times what it is like to stand judgingly between the opposites, one begins to understand what is meant by the self. Anyone who perceives his shadow and his light simultaneously sees himself from two sides and thus gets in the middle"*

*~ C. G. Jung*

Although it seems like the shadow self does not serve our spiritual journey, it is an important part of our growth towards self-love. In our human experiences are necessary life lessons that teach us about the value of divine love so we can embody this state of being. We must learn how to accept and understand the value and purpose of the opposing forces that tend to draw us away from authenticity. Part of our journey is learning how to come back to our true selves after the damaging mental conditioning by the world we long to be a part of. We are building spiritual strength with each experience in which we see beyond the mind programs. We need to live more from our higher minds that see these earthly challenges as compassionately solvable with self-love. This may be difficult when the fear is so debilitating, which draws us deeper into the darkness. That is why the shadow self was formed. It was there to contain in a shadowy space the needs and wants that are not in alignment with the expectations of the world, together with the emotional pain of rejection. We believe it would be safer to negate these natural parts of us so we can feel a sense of belonging in a world that can so easily negate our existence.

We learned from an early age that we must seek approval outside of ourselves in order find our worth. The shadow self allows us to hide those needy parts of ourselves so we can present a higher version of who we are to the world; someone who is confident, assertive, and emotionally stable. We allowed the ego mind to be our new truth, thereby denying our divinity.

When any part of us seeks control over the whole self, there is a disconnect in the layers of consciousness that make up the whole self. This means the layers cannot work in harmony, but instead oppose each other. This is also true for those that get so deep into spirituality that they want to rid themselves of the ego mind. The only way they can do that is by not engaging in the third dimensional realm. They would have to stay in a perpetual elevated level of consciousness which is difficult when dealing with everyday life.

As souls on a self-discovery journey, we are learning how to remain connected to the highest source of love and still have a physical experience of needs, wants and desires. We are being tested to see if we can stay true to our divine selves while we are faced with temptations of a lower vibration. You can think of it as a test to self-devotion. Since we are all collectively one with the All-Loving Creator, then a lack of devotion to ourselves as a divine source of love is a lack of devotion to the creation of all that is divine.

These temptations are judgment and criticism of others to make us feel better about ourselves, unscrupulously taking from others to build more for ourselves, projecting our emotional pain into the world to rid ourselves of it, overindulging in numbing substances, and seeking lust and sexual experiences in place of emotional depth. These lower vibrational experiences are due to a lack of self-love. They are due to soul traumas that caused the person to become controlled by their ego mind and live only for instant self-satisfaction. Their shadow self is filled with so much rejection that they must make their ego self strong, very much in charge and very much separate from the whole self.

Thankfully, most people are not so lost and disconnected from life, but they do continue to suppress parts of their true self into the shadows which prevents them from fully loving who they are. Suppression of our truest desires begins in childhood, and this is how the ego mind became the controlling force in our lives.

A young girl has a passion for toy trucks. Her mother's mind is conditioned to believe that little girls must play with little girl toys like dolls, tea sets and fluffy stuffed animals. Mother discourages her daughter from playing with the trucks by asserting that trucks are for boys. The little girl is confused because she wants to play with the trucks but also wants to please her mother. Pleasing mother is her way to ensure approval and acceptance. She must suppress her desire to play with the trucks and instead find an interest in what her mother deems proper for little girls. She not only has to shut this part of herself down, but she must also deny all parts of her that are called towards her love for trucks. Her false self begins to play with the toys her mother deems "girl toys." Although she may not feel as passionate during playtime, she feels safe, loved, and accepted by her mother. The authentic part of her is now deep within her shadow self and part of her passionate energy is suppressed along with it. She must reject this part of herself as a tradeoff for acceptance. She has suppressed the animus aspect of her soul –her innate masculine energy. This will keep her energetic body out of balance. Within the mind of the little girl is survival necessity that is stronger than her desire for trucks.

A man becomes a father for the first time. Although he is in awe of his new baby girl, he doesn't care to hold the infant. His father was emotionally distant and believed that babies are cared for by their mothers and the father's role is to financially support the family. This new father has been programmed to believe that men are not supposed to nurture babies or get emotionally connected to their children. This means he must suppress his anima aspect in order to adhere to what he believes is the role of the father.

A boy at the age of 12 finds himself romantically and sexually attracted to boys. He realizes his father could not accept him as a homosexual, so he must negate this desire. The part of him that is attracted to boys must be suppressed into the shadow to avoid humiliation by the public and abandonment by his father. He will grow up and marry a woman and continue to suppress his true desires. The boy's father is stuck in his conditioning that a man could and should only love a woman. This is now projected onto his son, causing the son to deny his natural tendencies. He is now in a fragmented state because he has pushed away a part of his true self. He must now live as his false self with a persona that he is happy in his marriage with a woman. The tradeoff is love and respect from his father.

A teenage girl gets called upon at school to answer a question. She tells the wrong answer and is humiliated in front of her class by the teacher who shouts out "wrong – it looks like someone didn't study." A boy yells out the correct answer and is praised for his knowledge and effort. The young girl immediately forms a belief that she is not as smart as the rest of the class. She shrieks in embarrassment and internally berates herself for her stupidity. She cannot handle the feelings of shame, so she suppresses this part of her. She unconsciously labels herself as lazy and incompetent. She must now create a false self that is motivated and always ready to learn. She exudes confidence and wisdom while another part of her feels inferior to the world.

All the people in these examples are experiencing internal conflicts between the ego self and the shadow self. This will keep them in a fragmented state and stagnated life if they do not reconcile the conflicts within them.

Although pushing our true desires and unhealed emotions out of conscious awareness causes stagnation later in life, it was a necessary survival strategy during childhood. Since the child's mind does not have the emotional maturity or proper coping mechanisms to work through hurtful emotions that negate their true self, the only way to continue to function in life was to ignore these debilitating feelings. By suppressing them out of awareness, the child was able to continue being a child without being overwhelmed by fear. What we did not know as children is that these emotions remain within us and contribute to how we navigate the rest of our lives.

We label our emotions as good or bad when all emotions are good. They provide us with information about where we stand on our journey. If we have buried emotions that we believe are bad, then we are not connecting to our true feelings, which leaves us trapped in our ego mind. There is wisdom in our wounds, and we must realize the benefit of experiencing the pain that leads us back to our divine truth.

There was a time when we had to suppress many of our childhood emotions. If we did not suppress the parts of us that we believe are flawed, then we would have a challenging time growing into adulthood. The child in you deserves praise for their acute survival skills. Now what they need is you, in your wise adult self, to help them out of the trap they got stuck in.

No matter what the strategy was at the time to avoid feeling pain, it allowed us to get to a temporary place of safety. If the child's mind could not find a way to fight against or escape the emotional trauma, the child's mind would eventually feel defeated by the emotional crisis and would lose the ability to adequately function in life. They would go into the freeze response where their nervous system shuts down for the time being because there is no escape from fear. Eventually, the emotions get suppressed and the nervous system relaxes, but the freeze response gets recorded by the nervous system as a go to strategy whenever a similar situation arises. The mind's ability to push these debilitating emotions below conscious awareness is a clever and tactical approach to feeling safe in a world that can feel quite threatening to a child. These survival strategies were a life saver in our earlier years. It does not serve us well as adults, but our childlike unconscious mind with unhealed emotional wounds conflicts with our grown-up logical view of life, causing the body to default to its childhood survival strategies, even into adulthood. This is because human nature is to first seek safety in any situation that feels threatening.

If we look back to the adult that caused the child to feel bad, we will be blaming the child part in the adult that did not heal from their trapped emotions. Just like the examples above, these children grew into adults living through a false self to avoid rejection by the world. The adults in their childhood years were doing the same. As they continue to function in life, those trapped emotions start surfacing and these well-adjusted adults go into childlike reactive behavior that gets projected onto the children they are caring for. Then the children blame themselves for causing the adult's reactive behavior and begin to feel ashamed and unworthy of the caregiver's love. The child is not aware that the adult was re-experiencing trauma from their childhood and their behavior was coming from the unhealed wounded child within them. Due to all the unhealed wounds in our ancestry, shadow work for inner child healing has become one of the most important and necessary healing modalities one can do for themselves.

Not all childhood experiences are dysfunctional. Some are quite normal, but the perceptions of the child were based in fear, causing the memories of certain situations to become distorted. As previously discussed, the child's mind is very imaginative and can create stories that do not match the situation. For example, if a parent tells a child that they are not focused enough when they play soccer, the child may instead hear the words "I am disappointed in you." Although these words were not spoken, the child may have a fear of disappointing their parents, so they misperceive the constructive criticism.

Many times, these misperceptions could cause a child to create a false self. The child may tell the parent that they no longer enjoy playing soccer. The child is trying to avoid further rejection. Their true self enjoys the sport but their false self, created by the protective ego, causes the child to believe that they have no interest in soccer. The child now has no love for the part of them that enjoyed the sport. The child's mind sees that part of them as unworthy, lousy at sports, and someone who cannot measure up to the other kids. This part of them must be rejected. As the child grows into adulthood and has children of their own, they may unconsciously deter their children from playing sports. The fear is that they will be seen as a failure and clumsy at sports. This is the adult's repressed inner child still locked in the fear of being a disappointment when it comes to sports. Although this part of the adult self is repressed, it still receives survival signals when triggered, causing the adult to create a safe space. The adult has unknowingly passed their fear of failure onto their children by discouraging them from engaging in the sport.

Our survival strategies from childhood were able to save us as children, but they have caused problematic disruptions in our lives as adults. We suffer from the fragmentation and disassociation of our genuine selves and do not realize how much we have placed limitations on our lives because of it and how we unconsciously pass our survival strategies onto those we love and care for.

There is an internal struggle in so many well-intentioned adults. The internal struggle is due to the need to be who we are and the need to be accepted in the world. We are afraid of disappointing others and fear being humiliated, judged, and rejected. These are all fears that stem from childhood. Whether our childhood was completely dysfunctional or whether we are just sensitive to the words and actions of others, the result is our limited love for ourselves.

We do not have to keep fighting with ourselves. The answer is to reconnect with our true selves by accepting these rejected parts of us that we buried a long time ago. We must realize that these childhood survival strategies are no longer needed as an adult. The adult mind knows how to work through tough times. The adult mind has logic, intelligence, wisdom, and a deeper understanding about life. When the adult mind is still being influenced by the overprotective ego mind, the adult will continue to keep their childhood wounds suppressed. They will not be living life as their genuine selves and will continue to rely on their fabricated persona to gain superficial approval by the world. This means they are still rejecting parts of themselves. They are still only loving the parts of themselves that they believe will not be rejected. They are still stuck in survival consciousness. This is not self-love. This is self-preservation.

The shadow self contains the parts of us that are true and unique, but emotionally undeveloped. We have much to learn about the repressed aspects of the whole self. We need to understand the value in being able to suppress them as children. We also need to see the value in creating a false self so we can gain acceptance into the world. These strategies to regain feelings of safety were more important to us than being our authentic selves. We need to forgive ourselves for choosing survival over our divine truth. It was necessary at the time, and we must accept this fact. We must also accept that now that we know better, we can do better. Self-love was not the priority during our most vulnerable years – survival was. This is all part of the journey to self-love. It is a letting go of our need for outside approval, so we can return to ourselves, but with a much higher understanding of love.

One of our biggest challenges is to learn how to love parts of ourselves that we label as flawed and unlovable. We had these beliefs for so long and felt safe in our false self. As wise adults, we want authentic love and the freedom to express who we are, while our ego has us seeking love through artificial means because it believes we have flawed aspects that must be hidden from the world. This is why we continue to remain in conflict with ourselves. These inner conflicts keep us from reaching and embodying the true meaning of self-love.

People that are egotistic or who live life only for material possessions are disconnected from love. They are filling the void with earthly possessions. They have no idea that they live in a place of self-denial. They do not see their value as they are. They must achieve something more to prove their worthiness to the world. Something went wrong for them as they were learning lessons. Something caused them to drift so far away from their true self that the emptiness made them hungry for love. They found that love through the security of having materialism. This is the false self that is compensating for the emptiness it feels from nonlove.

Another person may jump from one romantic relationship to another. They are seeking security, not love. This is their unhealed inner child that does not feel worthy of love because their caregivers' love was inconsistent and sometimes non-existent. This person is living through the false self because the true self that wants to love and be loved is trapped in the experience of rejection.

Someone may stay in a job that causes them immense stress because they believe they do not have sufficient skills to get higher-level employment. This part of the whole self is being controlled by their unhealed inner child who feels stupid and useless.

A young boy tries to help his dad with a home project. His dad tells him "stay away because you make it worse." The part of him that wanted to help had to be suppressed so he could avoid further disappointment. His false self will only take on small tasks to avoid disappointing others, which means avoiding rejection.

In all these scenarios, there is a rejection of the true self, deep feelings of unworthiness and possibly shame and fear of abandonment. There is an identification with the false self for survival purposes. We are all trying to avoid rejection and that is why the false self had to be created and why the false self remains the controlling force in life.

Most of us have self-rejected parts that cause the ego to step in and save us from our pain. In the experience of such pain, it felt like a death. We felt like we would be thrown to the wolves because we were so inadequate. The ego came to protect us, and we began to feel safe again.

The ego wants to eliminate our rejected parts as they cause a threat to the security of the whole self. No true part of us can be eradicated or destroyed. The strategic ego mind keeps them suppressed so they cannot be exposed to the world. Since so many people are still living through their false selves, this survival tactic has worked well.

Some people say their childhood memories are all good, their parents were incredibly supportive, and they felt loved. What they did not acknowledge is the friend group in middle school that ditched them, or the first love interest that cheated on them, or the neighborhood kid who bullied them. To a sensitive soul, these occurrences could cause a deep wound of unworthiness.

I do not know anyone, including myself, that has reached the level of authentic self-love. What I do know and what I want to emphasize in this book is that we are not expected to be living from our true selves from the beginning. We are expected to learn from the misguidance of ourselves and others, so that we can evolve into the highest version of ourselves and live in the higher truth.

During the physical journey, we have or will at some point in life, abandon our true self for the sake of approval and acceptance. It is part of our journey to realize who we are and come back to what Dr. Carl Jung calls the "Self."

In our authenticity, love is everything. It is our full and unhindered trust in the divine consciousness that lives within us. Creating the false self was an act of survival. Dissolving the false self is an act of self-love. When we gain enough trust in ourselves to be our true selves, then we will embody self-love. Until then, we are still learning as we journey through life. This is what we are supposed to do. We are here to learn, not deny, not separate our parts, but to gain wisdom through our experiences, whether they felt good, bad, or indifferent.

We may have much to learn, but if we are learning, then we are working towards self-love.

# Chapter 7

## The Ego as Our Protector

*"Until you transcend the ego, you can do nothing but add to the insanity of the world"*

*~ Wayne W. Dyer*

The English word "ego" is the Latin word "I." Ego gives us a sense of individual identity and helps us maintain a sense of control when it comes to our primitive desires. The ego helps us in our planning, strategizing and decision making. It gives us our perception of the external world and works to achieve a balance with our ethical and idealistic values.

Although the ego gets a bad rap at times, it really is an important part of our third-dimensional construct. It operates based on a reality principle and gives us the ability to interact with others and our environment. It also helps us identify and weigh out the consequences of our actions.

The ego can often be judgmental of others to protect itself. Since the ego is connected to one's identity, the ego loves to exhibit a sense of control over one's life, self-importance, and personal strength. It is also the part of us that works to keep us safe and free from judgment. The ego keeps us from acting out unacceptable traits in a social setting and helps us conform to the dictates of society so we can fit into this world. When someone is too much in their ego, they are trying too hard to avoid judgment and may even exhibit a grandiose attitude to overcompensate for insecurities.

The ego is not something we get rid of as many spiritual gurus have suggested. The ego is an important part of our personality for the reasons listed above. An ego problem only occurs when we cannot create a balance between the ego and the divine self. If we get stuck in egoism, which is being overly attentive to our own worldly needs and self-image, then we would be neglecting our authentic selves, which is the essence of our souls as created by the all-loving Creator. We would be denying our compassion and empathetic traits that help serve humanity. If we identify with the ego as who we are, then we are negating our true selves as we become more self-serving through our own unique beliefs, ideologies and judgements about others and the world. The ego believes that what we feel within has no effect on the world because we are separate and apart from all others. This is an illusion and defies our true mission on planet Earth. Everything we feel and think affects everything around us through its energetic signature.

Living in a judgmental world has caused many good souls to be controlled by the ego mind, causing spiritually depleted human beings. The purpose of ego was to give us an identity of "I" and allow us to function in the third-dimensional world with the ability to interact with others on a conscious level. We were not meant to negate our divine nature. We were meant to experience what it feels like to be disconnected from love so we could appreciate the value of love and claim it as our healing source for difficult earthly challenges. Instead, many people have allowed their ego to become their power source because they feel disconnected from themselves. The outer world becomes the problem-solving source, and the inner world of personal thoughts, feelings and emotions are ignored. What is not realized by the ego mind is that the inner world is what helps to create the outer world. This is why people with strong egos have many challenges in life. They are not tapping into their inner source of love to help heal their disconnect from themselves because their focus is mostly on survival, which is the need to have control over how the outer world receives them.

A healthy ego does not harshly judge others but may make healthy observations about people or situations. A healthy ego is balanced with the divine self and knows when it needs to be prominent and when to put its trust in spirit – the divine self. The unhealthy ego wants to stand in power over the whole self so it can protect it from judgment by others while it projects onto others the very criticisms they fear about themselves. The healthy, balanced consciousness of the whole self understands that some people are trapped in their pain, causing them to rely more on ego and survival consciousness than their true self. A balanced Self knows that many people are not in touch with their divine energy because of the many soul traumas they have endured during their physical journey. If we judge them for not being able to show love, then we are in judgment, which means we are giving power to our ego mind. We cannot be in judgment of others while also being in a place of self-love since self-love is an embodied consciousness that can only project out love energy. This does not mean that there won't be challenging times even for those that have done the deep healing work. The difference is how to react or respond to others and the world during such difficult times.

For our lives to feel balanced, we must understand that there are natural parts of our psychological makeup that may go off balance. When this happens, our bodies feel disharmony and tension. To return to balance, we need to check in with our ego mind. The divine self already knows the higher truth. If we give too much power to the ego, then we are not trusting who we really are. This could cause the divine self to shrink down and allow the ego mind to take control. We have a much greater purpose than feeding the ego self.

The ego does not like losing control over the outside world, but it does not realize that it never had control. To let go of trying to control life and just be with life is quite scary to the ego mind. I do not want to say we need an ego death to raise our consciousness, which you may hear in many spiritual teachings; it is more like ego transcendence. Ego transcendence is going beyond the concern for oneself. It is seeing the bigger reality. Seeing the bigger reality comes from seeing the bigger picture around the problems the ego tries to control. By seeing the bigger picture and the purpose of our life challenges, then we can appreciate the lessons we are here to learn instead of getting stuck in the pain of them. This means learning the spiritual lessons behind our challenges and realizing that the only remedy is authentic love.

The development of the ego takes place during young childhood. It comes in strong as a protector over the whole self, but now we are trying to tame it down so we can live more in our divine energy and travel the path to authentic self-love. We may have become too reliant on ego, as it does prevent us from seeing the parts of us that we believe are inferior and places us above our perceived flaws so we can feel accepted by the world. The fear of letting the ego relax is due to the fear of losing these protections. This means we must learn how to trust ourselves in our divine truth. If the world has been particularly challenging for us, then it could be a difficult process to relax the ego that has artificially protected us for so long.

Bringing the ego into balance is the only way to stop living from a false self. Having an overprotective ego keeps us from doing many great things. It holds us back from experiencing a full life and keeps us on high alert as we navigate our environment. This keeps the body in a stressful state and the mind preoccupied with proving our worth to the world.

Ego is a part of our third-dimensional structure that may need to come into play when you are dealing with the material world. It is not here to fight with the world; it is here to engage with the world in a very mature and natural way. When we finally integrate all the energies and come back into balance, the ego will stop over protecting the whole self and settle into its supportive role as a deliberate organizer for the highest good of the whole self and humanity.

The ego can be a little intimidated when we step fully into self-love because it feels like it is losing its power. You want the ego to understand that it is not being dissolved; it is being brought into harmony with the higher truth.

The ego can be described as one's self-esteem. It is the ego mind that helps us be strong, capable human beings in many aspects of our lives. The ego gives us a sense of self-importance. Although many spiritual gurus believe the ego causes separation, it is that separation that gives us our individual free will. We came here as separate beings so we can experience our individual souls and learn the value of love from each other. The only way to learn this is to experience the pain in our souls when we do not embody self-love. The spark of God's light within us connects our souls to the collective body of light where we are unified love consciousness. We are here to learn how to stay in that integration of love, even though we have the free will to turn away from love and possibly cause harm to others. We are here to learn how to make choices that align with our mission to bring love and peace to the world.

The ego sets up protector parts that stand guard over our vulnerable parts so we can function in life without fear. Protector parts work around the clock to ensure that your wounded childhood parts are never exposed to the world. These protector parts stepped into protective action when you were very young and did not have the resources to cope with emotionally challenging situations. These protectors continue to protect these childhood parts even in your adulthood, so they have been with you for a long time. Protectors are not trying to hold you back. They only want to ensure that you do not re-experience your pain.

Suppose as a child, you wanted safety from abandonment because your dad left the home when you were seven years old. Your body began to quiver and then feel weak. It is like your world was crashing in on you. The emotions were so overwhelming that the ego believed you were dying. Remember, the ego is all about survival. To keep you alive and safe, the ego suppresses these intense emotions and blocks the fearful thoughts around them. As an adult, you do not realize that these suppressed emotions are affecting your decisions when it comes to important relationships. You may find yourself getting nervous around your romantic partnerships and your body starts to quiver like it did in the past. You may feel weak or anxious as you feel more connected to your partner, so you unconsciously sabotage the relationship. You may avoid relationships altogether. You may believe you are having bad luck in love or that there is something off with the partners you choose. You cannot see how you caused the destruction of the relationship or how you may keep yourself at a distance from potential partners. You are not aware of the deep hidden fears of abandonment that have been suppressed within you since you were seven years old.

The quivering of the body comes from the shock to the nervous system from the first feelings of abandonment. The body may feel weak and exhausted from emotional stress. The conscious mind will not be able to interpret the body's reaction and may be bewildered by the uneasy feelings. This keeps the young child, right into adulthood, stuck in an unhealthy pattern that can be described as "love avoidant." This was not the intention of the protector parts. They serve the whole self, but their biggest concern is safety.

It may seem like protector parts want to do more harm than good. The truth is they only want to do good. They want the whole self to be able to feel safe in the world. When a part of the whole self becomes debilitated because of fear of abandonment, the whole self suffers.

Protector parts will go to great lengths to keep us feeling safe and acceptable to the world. These protector parts will keep all shadow parts in the shadows, out of conscious awareness and hidden from society. Protector parts will rely on the ego mind to ensure continued safety and acceptance. The young lady who avoids intimate relationships because of an unconscious fear of abandonment is now living through a false self. She believes her relationship issues are outside of herself. She is being influenced by an incomplete trauma. The only way she can complete the trauma is to feel safe again. The only way she can feel safe in relationships is to heal the past relationship that shattered her heart. She cannot do that if her ego keeps her from acknowledging the unhealed pain. When someone needs to heal a painful relationship from the past, it does not mean that they need to heal with that person. They need to heal the disconnect to self-love and self-acceptance caused by the relationship rupture.

Our protector parts keep us from healing our suppressed wounds because of the strong walls they placed around them. They take their job quite seriously and do not give in so easily. Protector parts need to be gently coaxed to let anyone, including us, get close to them. This can take time since protector parts do not want to give up the job they were called to do by the ego.

By working with protector parts with love and compassion, we may get them to soften while we work with our wounded parts. We are not taking away the job of the protector as they are a part of the ego mind. We are simply bypassing it to help ourselves heal childhood wounds that keep us from loving who we are.

Once our wounded parts are given the opportunity to heal the pain and release the fears they carry, the protectors can relax. There will no longer be an old wound to protect or a threat against a vulnerable part of the whole self. Protector parts will continue to protect the whole self, but from a more mature consciousness and against current threats, not imagined ones that stem from old childhood wounding still playing out in the unconscious mind.

This is a process that is worth the time and effort to complete because it will bring peace to the whole self, which means the person can now drop the false self and live in wholeness as the Self. This will lead to authentic self-love.

# Chapter 8

## When Love is Limited

*"The spiritual journey is the unlearning of fear and the acceptance of love"*

*~ Marianne Williamson*

One of the biggest barriers to self-love is not having a connection to people who accept us in our authenticity. When we are unable to express ourselves from our truth, we remain stuck in our false selves for acceptance. Dr. Gabor Mate, a Canadian physician, who has an interest in child development, says "People have two needs: Attachment and authenticity. When authenticity threatens attachment, attachment trumps authenticity." This means if being our true selves will result in rejection by people we are attached to, then we feel safer suppressing our authenticity. People will have a difficult time accepting us as we are if they can't accept themselves as they are. The fear of being rejected causes us to limit the love we have for ourselves because we do not love the parts of us that are true to who we are.

When we limit the love that we have for ourselves, we also limit the love we have for others. This is because we can only love others as much as we love ourselves. We hold back parts of our authentic self which means we are holding back genuine love. These suppressed parts of us are from the divine consciousness of love and compassion. If we are rejecting them as inferior because we believe they are unworthy, then the love they embody is also suppressed.

When we live life through our persona instead of our genuine selves, we are not expressing love from a genuine place. We are only expressing our need for love because we feel so unlovable. We do not realize that we are lovable because we have already deemed parts of us as not worthy of love. This causes us to seek out love in ways that are not authentic love. They are safety conditions disguised as love. We cannot be in survival consciousness and live a life of divine truth at the same time.

If we have suppressed our need for affection because it was never provided to us during our childhood, we may seek out romantic partners that are unaffectionate. This is the shadow part of us that is rejecting affection because it feels undeserving to us. We believe we love them fully, but we cannot love the part of them that is unaffectionate. We are naturally affectionate, loving, intimate beings. We do not realize that we brought these childhood survival strategies into our adult relationships. The attraction towards someone who is unaffectionate is security disguised as love. It is that unhealed part of us that believes the need for affection is wrong.

Authentic love comes from the heart. The heart center connects us to the soul where we long to be in our natural divine energy. We can only authentically love ourselves and others through this divine energy which represents our true selves. We are not living through our true selves when we are still being held back by our unresolved childhood wounding.

Sometimes we seek out our rejected parts in others. This means that if we rejected our natural urge for affection due to childhood programming, we may seek out partners who are overly affectionate. This is us attempting to reclaim our lost parts. Even though we are reclaiming our split-off energies, we are doing it through others which is not conducive to balancing our energies. We must balance them within ourselves.

This physical journey has challenged many of us and the goal is to come back to love. We come in with love and when we feel a sense of losing love, we go into fear response because we need the love to survive in the physical world. We then try to control love by living through the ego mind. Love is not something you control. When we are in the internal state of love, we are openly expressing love and open to receiving the love we know we deserve. This is not something the false self can comprehend. The false self seeks security and situations that will meet our childhood needs, so that the whole self can feel significant enough to be accepted in this world. This is the biggest disconnect to our divine power. We have given it up to ego because we are stuck in our childhood programming of unworthiness and our need for survival.

A soul that feels fragmented cannot genuinely love another whole-heartedly. The soul feels broken and unworthy. This causes the soul to meet the needs of the ego so that the whole self can be at peace. What is not known is that by living through a persona, we conflict with our true divine selves which means we are not at peace – we just pretend to be.

If we continue to limit the love for ourselves, we will continue to limit our love for others. If we keep disguising security as love, then we will feel it energetically. We will feel unbalanced and fragmented causing us to keep seeking those missing parts through others. We will be negating our very nature to love ourselves and others unconditionally. We do not realize how much we hold back, which then causes others to hold back. This leads to more emotional frustration as we continue to seek security instead of love.

We are all capable of loving ourselves and others to the highest level, but since we feel broken and insecure, we do not reach that level of self-love which allows us to unconditionally love others.

If we want to fully engage with the energy of self-love, we will need to release the false self and trust that our genuine self is worthy of the world no matter how judgmental it is. When we accept and integrate our rejected parts, we will not be concerned what the world thinks of us because we will already know who we are. We will be able to accept our uniqueness and individuality, even if someone else does not. We will already understand, from a higher level of consciousness, that many people do not accept themselves and may project their unconscious self-disdain onto us. This may require us to forgive ourselves for not knowing that we deserve authentic love and forgive others for not being in alignment with love when we wanted their acceptance.

We want to love others with all the love we can give, and we do. We give love equal to the love we allow ourselves to receive. We do not allow the parts of us that we rejected to receive love. If we disowned parts of ourselves, then we cannot feel whole. If we do not feel whole, then we cannot love others with our whole self, only with a partial self which means partial love. Even though we feel less than whole, we are never less than whole, and we are not separate from our rejected parts. We just feel fragmented because we are not in touch with all our parts, because much of our true selves are sitting in the shadows of who we are.

When we feel fragmented, we are lacking balance in our energies. This makes us want to seek balance through others. This is not loving them. This is pulling on their energy so we can feel stable. We will always seek love outside of ourselves when we feel a lack of love within ourselves. If we are seeking it, then we do not feel complete in it. When we embody self-love, authentic love comes into our lives.

We are all on a journey to discover the truth about ourselves. We have been living through third dimensional mind programs because we do not know anything else. Some of us may need more time to find our authenticity, especially if childhood experiences have caused confusion and feelings of unworthiness. This takes deep inner work, which is an act of self-love. When we reach that divine space within ourselves, we will realize how we became trapped in our ego minds and sought security over love. We can forgive ourselves for seeking out false love because we did what we needed to do at the time – which is survive. Now, we can give ourselves permission to live like the miracles we are because we have gained wisdom, knowledge and a deeper understanding of human consciousness.

The truth is that we can fully embody the highest love because we are made from the energy of the All-Loving Creator. When we have disowned parts of our true selves, we have disowned parts of this energy. Our true nature is that of the spirit. The physical body is the container that allows us to experience this physical world and explore the physical manifestations of love.

The unfortunate truth about experiencing nonlove is that we turn against ourselves as a punishment for not measuring up to the expectations of society. When we turn on ourselves, we tend to unknowingly hurt others. For example: A man who grew up feeling heavily criticized no matter how hard he tried to be the good little boy for his parents unconsciously craves acceptance as an adult. While at work, his boss criticizes him for not completing a project in a timely manner. The man shrinks in shame and holds in his anger and resentment for what he feels is unwarranted criticism. He heads home at the close of business and finds himself sitting in traffic as he is seething with anger and despair. He cannot stop thinking about how he has failed again. His thoughts are self-criticizing, self-sabotaging and filled with deep anguish about his abilities to be accepted by a judgmental world. He is confirming everything his primary caregivers made him feel as a child. He finally gets home after a long day of feeling emotionally distraught, unlovable and insignificant. The emotional stress is too much to bear, so he releases his rage onto his wife and child. Now the wife and child are questioning their worthiness. This is how feelings of unworthiness keep trekking through the familial line. In this moment, the love is limited towards his family because he lost himself in the fear of unworthiness and unknowingly passed this pain onto the people he loves. Since he has not healed his insecurities from childhood, the love for his family has been limited from the beginning. It is not that he doesn't love his wife and child, but he is holding back love from himself, so he cannot fully love others unless he feels whole.

We must pull ourselves out of this unworthiness trap. If we do not, we will keep losing ourselves in the pain and fear of rejection instead of following our true divine mission of embodying love even when we experience the fear of nonlove. It is not easy, but we are learning. Some of us are learning faster than others, and that simply means we must be the example of self-love. Does this man's wife and child realize that this is not about them? Most likely not. They will now carry this pain within them because as they were seeking love and acceptance from their loved one, they instead felt a deep sense of rejection.

As adults, many of us are now learning how to return to who we really are. It is called "the awakening" and we all experience this awakening when we are ready to accept the higher truth. The awakening is when we see our divine value and no longer hold onto those old patterns that keep us from loving ourselves and others. The awakening is a process and many of us are going through it now. We are coming back to ourselves. We are working towards loving ourselves even though we experienced so many situations that felt like nonlove. The more we understand human consciousness, the fears that can take over the mind and the reason we got so trapped in our pain, the easier it will be to embrace this awakening. If we remain stuck in confusion and cannot release old survival patterns, then we will miss out on the greatest expansion of consciousness that is now being experienced on this planet. We can no longer be afraid. We must  be brave enough to enter those lower levels of the mind and bring them the healing power of our higher mind. Love is always the divine answer to the fears of unworthiness that we experience on this journey.

We cannot limit our love. It causes pain and keeps us in a collective body of fear. We need to support this ascension for ourselves and for humanity. We need to create change and the only way to do that is to realize that holding onto the fear of not being enough is preventing us from implementing our divine mission on planet Earth. Join the souls that are calling for the higher truth to be globally recognized. Be part of the mission that you were called here to participate in. Do not let fear win. Do not let those trapped feelings of unworthiness affect who you are and what you are capable of. Do not limit your love for yourself and others because you have experienced trauma. Most of the world has experienced some level of trauma. Be the light for others while they learn how to seek the light within themselves. As you hold the light for others, do not let yourself absorb their energy. Protect your light by staying in the vibration of the higher truth. Your light will shine upon them simply because you embody it. By being your true self, you help others learn how to let go of the false self they have become comfortable with.

# Chapter 9

## Releasing and Grieving the False Self

*"Your false self requires seeking, your true self does not"*

*~ Kyle Hoobin*

When we have become accustomed to living through our false self, we become attached to this version of ourselves. This is the persona that helped us earn the praise, love, attention, and affection we needed and wanted. To change who we believe we are means letting go of the security that the persona provided.

Human beings are always seeking to get their needs met and creating a persona that helps them do that is not going to be so easily released. This is because releasing familiarity so we can grow and expand our consciousness opens the door to the unknown. Entering the door of the unknown pulls us back to survival mode if the change feels uneasy. It seems like we can be caught in between living our lives authentically without fear of judgment or playing it safe within our familiar comfort zone and being content with our limited lives. It is not an easy choice for the human mind because the ego is seeking safety through the false self, and the soul is seeking expansion through these human experiences.

As human beings, we direct most of our energy towards security and leaving this feeling of safety can be difficult. To release the aspects of the false self requires us to go through a grieving process that can cause havoc on the emotional and physical bodies. As we begin to connect more with our authentic selves, we shed the layers of the false self. We can feel our bodies releasing those contracted energies that keep pulling us back to survival mode. This can feel scary, draining and sometimes debilitating because the body has been in a contracted state for a long time. The nervous system is conditioned to go into a fight, flight or freeze response when triggered and the survival brain has us stuck on high alert. We may not have noticed this because our physical bodies are accustomed to these sensations. When we start to breakdown the false self, we will feel like we are going through a death and a rebirth. This is a big adjustment after years of self-protection.

Releasing the old self means grieving what you thought was you and letting go of the need for approval. When we are trapped in the ego mind, we rely on the approval and acceptance of others to keep our ego alive. The ego believes death of the ego is death of the physical self. The ego does not know that you are a divine being and there is no such thing as death – only transformation. The ego self needs to be convinced that it is safe to release the false self and welcome back the aspects of whole self that were rejected as self-protection. This is a huge change for the whole self, but the return to the authentic self is the ultimate reward for this healing and integration. When you go through a transformation, you are not letting go of any parts of you that belong to your true divine self. You are only releasing the parts of you that have been created by the ego mind to fit in with the world. You do not have to fit in. You just need to spread love and peace and the world will respond to you with that same frequency. The people that do not fit into your world of authenticity are not ready for you and that is OK. Your caregivers were probably not ready for you either because they were still experiencing their trauma wounds.

When you are ready to let go of the false self, you might feel some resistance coming from the ego mind. The ego mind does not want to give up its job of protecting the whole self. The ego mind believes that without this protection, the whole self becomes vulnerable to the rejection of others because of its inferior parts. This is the illusion that must be exposed and dissolved. You have an intelligent and rational mind, intuition, and spiritual support from your Creator when you are ready to become aware of your divine truth. Most importantly, you have a heart that feels deep love for the younger versions of you that have been rejected. You closed your heart to these parts of you so you could function in life through your most vulnerable years. You are older and wiser now and you are learning that your false self does not align with your soul's purpose. Your soul knows it did not come here to fit in. Your soul came here to experience love and the consequences of not choosing love. The moment you feared that love was lost, you began to worry about your purpose here and started relying on others to give you purpose. This has caused you to rely on your ego mind to gain a feeling of belonging and significance. This has been a deception of the mind since you were young. Now you are being asked to let this all go and step into an unknown reality. The truth is you are not stepping into the unknown. You are returning to the divine truth that you came from. You are returning to your authentic self.

When you release the false self and fully grieve the old patterns, you may find yourself stepping away from certain people in your life. Once you raise your energy level to a divine love frequency, it will be difficult to spend time with those that project a strong ego mind, including those that you have relied on for your emotional and physical needs. If this causes any feelings of guilt, you may need to remind yourself that you are not abandoning anyone, you are simply returning to Self.

It is uncomfortable for the soul when the ego mind feels the need to pretend who the whole self is. Keeping up the pretense can be emotionally and physically exhausting, as the fears of being found out are always lurking in the back of the mind. Breaking down the false self means revealing the true self, which can sometimes upset those that benefitted from us as our false self.

The true self is a being of love and compassion, but also one with a healthy ego. There could be personality clashes between two healthy egos, but the true self would have the maturity level to stand true to their opinions and values, while also respecting the opinions and values of others. Most of us do not meet our true selves until we are adults and have healed and integrated our shadow parts, grieved and released the false self, and established a practical ego. We need to be patient with the process of releasing those old familiar patterns and trust that we will be safe when we live from the heart instead of the protective ego.

Since most of us have experienced some level of dysfunction or fear of nonlove during our growing up years, we must find a way to feel safe enough to remove the mask that we wore for so long; the mask that made us feel validated. This will take some inner work and many of us have become so comfortable with our persona that we do not believe we need to do the work.

Releasing and grieving your false self is a process that is worth going through. Coming back to your true self means you accept who you are even if others do not. Not everyone will like the true you, and not everyone will like the false you. What is important is self-love. If you do not love all parts of you, then you will never feel balanced. That is not a favorable way to journey through life. It steals your joy and keeps you on hyper-alert to ensure no one can see your (perceived) inferior parts. Although releasing and grieving the old you can be uncomfortable, it will lead you back to authentic self-love, which is what we all have been striving for in this lifetime.

When we were children, we only knew how to express who we are. We came into this world to be our true selves. What we needed were teachers that acted from their true self. Since that was quite rare, we are all stuck in the same trap. We were not allowed to be ourselves because the people before us were not allowed to be who they were. Now we are learning how to come back to us. The only way to really let the past go is to know our past. We cannot know it completely if much of it is suppressed. By letting go of the false self and trusting that those suppressed parts are just innocent child parts that need love, we will be able to give them what they need and fully integrate them back into our lives. We can reach those suppressed parts of us simply by relaxing our minds and letting ourselves drift inward. As we focus on love, we can call upon the parts of us that need our love.

# Chapter 10

## Generational Trauma and the Shadow Self

*"By developing a relationship with the painful parts of ourselves— parts we have often inherited from our family—we have an opportunity to shift them. Qualities like cruelty can become the source of our kindness; our judgments can forge the foundation of our compassion"*

*~ Mark Wolynn*

The world is like a projector because many people in the world, without conscious awareness, are projecting their disowned shadow parts onto others. Everything that they rejected within themselves are unconsciously getting projected onto others as if the other has these issues, personality traits or inadequacies. This is because they want to believe that it exists *out there* and not within them. For example, a woman has a shadow aspect which represents a younger version of herself who feels unattractive. Her younger self was told that she has an awkward appeal to her. As a young girl she perceives this to mean that she is not attractive enough for the world. To protect herself from feeling deficient and unworthy of love, she rejects this part of herself, along with feelings of unworthiness. During her teenage years, she criticizes many girls for their appearance. She then creates a false self that becomes obsessed with everything that represents the social acceptance of beauty. Her shadow self is a little girl who feels unlovable, unwanted, and aesthetically inadequate. As a young adult, she persistently tells her female friends how they should dress, wear their hair, and do their makeup so they could be more attractive to others. In her unconscious mind are the thoughts that our value comes from how the world sees us esthetically. This can be hurtful to others and taken as criticism towards their appearance.

What she is unconsciously doing is judging her shadow aspect. She is projecting onto others what she cannot accept within herself. She needs to make her friends feel that they are not pretty enough as they are, when it is the younger version of herself trapped in the shadows that feels this way.

As small children, we believed that the projections of others were an indication of our identity, worthiness, significance, and lovability. The truth is that they are an indication of the unhealed pain within the one doing the projecting. We may understand this from our adult logical mind, but children do not have that intellectual capacity. Whatever you tell a child becomes the truth for them. They have no reason to believe anyone would lie to them. When children are very young, they do not know lying exists. They only feel that it is necessary to bond with the people who care for them no matter what that takes.

As adults, within us is that unhealed inner child who is getting triggered by the projections of others. As others are projecting their shadow aspects, they are triggering the feelings of unworthiness of those around them. Every time we re-experience the pain of the past, we begin to question our safety and value in the world. We may take the projections of others quite personally, causing a survival response. We may shut down (freeze response) because we cannot remove ourselves from the triggering situation. We may react with anger (fight response) or we may separate ourselves (flight response) from the person who triggered us. When triggered, our unconscious mind seeks safety first.

Although these survival responses may seem irrational, they are quite normal. We are hard-wired to seek safety whenever we feel a threat to our well-being. Our well-being feels secure if we believe we are "good enough" to exist in this world. An action or inaction that is hurtful in some way, can cause a reactivation of emotions that were buried many years earlier. These old childhood memories keep reminding us how we are a disappointment to those caring for us. The unconscious mind immediately recalls the survival strategy used by the child when they first felt those emotions and reactivates that same survival response. Since all the reactions come from the unconscious mind which then triggers the nervous system, there is no logic connected to the reactive response. There is only a fear response that seems irrational for the current circumstances. What is not recognized at the time is that the body is holding the memory of the past and that is why the current situation seems so extreme. It was an intense time for the child who did not have the ability to cope with a fearful situation that is still being processed through the adult. For the situation to be fully processed, the adult must address the painful feelings of the child.

The child's mind is always seeking acceptance and validation. When anything threatens that, there will be an immediate survival response. The survival response and underlying emotions do not mitigate over time. They just stay dormant until something causes a reactivation. As adults, not only do we get triggered by others, but many times we are unknowingly triggering others as we unconsciously project our shadow parts. The people we are closest to experience our shadow aspects the most. Many times, it is because we seek connection with them and when we feel the connection being threatened, we become anxious, and our shadow aspects go into protection mode. The result is a projection of our fears onto our loved ones. We are hard-wired for human connection. Our ancestors belonged to tribes where they worked together as a unit for survival purposes. We are much more civilized today, but we carry those survival traits within us.

If we feel a disconnect within our tribal unit, meaning our family, then we can experience the fear of not belonging and, therefore, not safe. In our adult lives, this may cause us to question our ability to connect deeply with others which then keeps us from fulfilling our natural humanistic need of tribal connection. The fear of rejection lives within all of us and we will do whatever it takes to avoid it, even if it means rejecting our need for deep intimate connections and accepting superficial relationships. We may then project our fear of not belonging onto others which may cause them to also fear deep intimate connections. This is generational trauma and there seems to be no end to it unless we heal the fears from the past and direct our energy towards self-love instead of these primitive survival responses. This means we must work with the suppressed emotions that keep the nervous system on high alert. A feeling of disconnect occurs when we feel disrespected, betrayed, abandoned, unloved or unwanted by someone in our tribe that is relevant to our survival, usually our parents. These memories then cause us to unconsciously react in a similar way to our own children. These projections are automatic and can sometimes seem quite harsh to others. Unfortunately, there does not seem to be much control over what triggers us unless we heal the fears and emotions underneath our unconscious reactive behaviors.

We can say society, as a whole, is responsible for so many problems in the world. Emotions play a big part in our mental health. When there are so many emotionally unstable people in the world, it can only create more instability. To help heal this societal crisis, it starts with each one of us.

Since many people are unaware of their internal suffering, generational trauma remains a big issue when it comes to emotional well-being. Many people are not doing the necessary healing work that will bring them back to energetic balance. Instead, they are living through the false self with a false sense of safety controlled by the ego mind. They find other ways to compensate for where they feel deficient because the goal is to ensure acceptance by the tribe to create feelings of significance and safety. This can certainly lead to over pleasing others to avoid further rejection, keeping them in survival-love instead of self-love. When the goal is not self-love, but outside validation, then the ego mind is the one driving the life of the soul. This can only cause more ego-driven people in the world. Our antiquated safety mechanisms are keeping us from living through our divine consciousness and experiencing authentic love. When we become bound to each other through fear instead of love, we lose our genuine selves to the ego mind of survival.

Although we may logically know and understand that we are not to blame for the unhealed trauma of another, the child parts that live within us have not reached that level of maturity. They are still blaming themselves for not being enough. When the inner child becomes triggered, it is once again looking at its insufficient self which could cause a survival response in the adult self. The adult does not realize that it is a childhood part of them that was triggered by a memory. They automatically assume that the current environment is the problem. The adult's reactive behavior now becomes an indelible mark upon the children they care for who will keep the original trauma, which can go back many generations, in full force. Although these ancestral traumas will show up differently in everyone they affect, they are nonetheless an old survival pattern that seems to be ongoing only because no one has done the inner work to halt its progression.

As more people rely on the ego for safety and acceptance, the longer generational trauma will exist and cause more emotional issues for humanity. Does this mean we live in an egotistical society? No; it means we live in a world that does not know how to properly heal because they have no awareness of their deeply hidden wounds. Their false selves have replaced their true selves, and they are not aware of the impact this has on their souls and society. They do not have a spiritual connection to themselves and that is why they feel a sense of separation from love. It is the love they have for themselves that is buried along with their shadow aspects.

Without awareness, people with unhealed emotional traumas are imprinting their hidden wounds onto those they care for, which is mostly young innocent children. When these children grow up, they become adults with hidden aspects of shame that get projected onto others. We are caught in ongoing cycles of projected emotional trauma and there does not seem to be much change in that. When we fail ourselves, we fail others, including our loved ones. By continuously seeking the remedy for our self-rejection outside of us, we continue to ignore what is inside of us.

Everyone who has suppressed emotional trauma was once that child that only wanted to be loved and accepted. This includes the wounded inner child of those adults that were unable to properly parent their children. They tried, but they failed because they did not know how to parent differently. They had their own beliefs based on their upbringing, along with trapped emotional trauma that would surface when a trigger set it off. When they projected their pain outward, they did not realize that the child in them was trying to free themselves from the heaviness of their trauma.

The only way to stop generational trauma in its tracks is by being the cycle breaker of our ancestry. We can do the inner healing work that others were not able to do. We can be the ones to break the chain of emotional trauma that keeps our loved ones from experiencing authentic self-love. By healing our own shadow parts and stepping into the higher truth of who we are in these human suits, we create significant changes not only in ourselves, but also in the world.

If we become responsible for our own healing instead of seeking the cure outside of ourselves, we will come back to our divine truth and live from a higher level of awareness. This is how we reach authentic self-love – that divine space and spiritual power that no one and nothing can take from us. In this higher love octave, we spread the energy of love and healing. When we do inner work individually, we help create a kinder world.

It is important to remember that we have absorbed some of the energy of our ancestry. They did not directly project their shadow wounds onto us, but through the transfer of cellular memory, we absorbed the energy of how they felt about themselves and the world they experienced during their lifetime.

Our ancestors had to endure some very traumatic events including famines, severe poverty, incurable diseases, world wars, restrictive cultures, and annihilation of certain ethnic groups. Their survival fears got passed down through the generations. Although we are a whole new and different generation, we still carry survival consciousness and are still seeking to get our emotional needs met. This is because many of those that came before us did not get their emotional needs met and their unhealed wounds passed through the generations. This causes us to experience the same feelings of inadequacy which we may have, unknowingly and innocently, passed onto others.

We have made great strides over the generations, but we continue to feel judged by others for our ethnicity, race, appearance, intelligence, career, and financial status. Since generations past did not have the healing opportunities we have today, they suffered in silence. Even as an advanced society, we keep questioning our safety and value in the world.

All the pain and fear that humans must endure during their physical journey are keeping the world in a state of chaos. As a collective body of energy, we contribute to the vibration of the planet. If we are in a low vibrational state, then that is the energy we will contribute to the world. If the collective vibration of the planet is low, then we will experience more world chaos. Our collective consciousness has an impact on the atmosphere where we live and wish to thrive. Unfortunately, it is difficult to thrive when the energy around us feels so heavy and uninspiring.

Most people do not do the inner healing work because they have placed thick, heavy walls over their hearts and continue to function in life through their persona. They are unaware that inner healing work would give them back their peace and emotional freedom. They continue to seek safety as their love source and create unhealthy distractions to hide from their pain. Since so many people believe the false self is their true authentic self, they do not see any reason to change or do not believe they can.

We might view others as appearing whole and balanced because of the way they appear to us. What we do not see are those hidden parts they hold in shame. The man who makes it to the top of the corporate ladder, but cannot find fulfillment in a romantic relationship, put all his energy into his career to avoid his fear of nonlove. He passes onto his children the belief that money takes priority over quality time with loved ones. The children bury within the shadow self their need for dad's love and attention. They grow up as a carbon copy of dad, chasing money and neglecting love. They pass the same onto their children, causing them to feel unworthy of love. Society will praise this man for his commitment to his goals, and yet, he feels fragmented and alone. We also do not realize the detrimental effect it has on those he can influence. The praise gives his ego a big boost and keeps him satiated for a while. When those shadow feelings surface, he finds a way to avoid, distract from or numb these feelings. Since no one is doing any inner work to heal the pain of nonlove, this familial line will continue to live through their egos, although their souls ache for love. Some of these family members will criticize people who spend too much time with family instead of building their fortune. This would be a projection. They are criticizing their inner child who wants more love, attention, and affection from their family. The ego believes financial status is more important because it ensures acceptance and survival, where love and affection invite criticism and rejection.

The woman who puts all her energy into caring for her spouse and neglects herself because of lack of boundaries and people pleasing traits is seen as the selfless and dedicated wife. We do not see the painful fears of unworthiness that live within her shadow self. As a child, she was bullied by her brother and always felt like she could not do enough to win his love and respect. Since she is holding back love from herself due to feelings of unworthiness, she lives through the survival consciousness she learned as a child. She is not experiencing authentic love. This means she cannot express authentic love towards her husband. Parts of her are being held back in the shadow self. Instead, she directs all her energy into caring for her husband to prove to him she is good enough to be loved and accepted by him. Her husband is her survival source. She does not realize that this is the real attraction. Authentic love comes from an open heart, higher awareness, and divine truth. Her heart is closed for protection, and she is not aware that she is more in her survival energy than her love energy.

We cannot fake authentic love. It has its own vibrational signature and is felt energetically by others. Most people have not experienced authentic love, so they are satisfied with superficial intimate connections.

We lost the spiritual essence of the human self when we gave our power to the ego. Now we seek to regain our spiritual essence through outside spiritual practices. We must look within ourselves first. That is where our spiritual truths are. If we rely on spiritual practices, which are high level coping mechanisms if we have not done the inner work, we will continue to keep generational trauma alive. They may not be big traumas, but just enough of a disconnect to the self to cause the ego to take the reigns and create a false identity for protection.

It is natural and our birthright to experience authentic love. This can only come from a higher level of awareness. It takes work to deprogram our conditioned minds, but it is worth it. The energy of deep spiritual self-love that is experienced when we step out of the fears of nonlove and fully into the Self is like pulling ourselves out of quicksand and walking towards the sun. Many of us are ready for this transformation. Since you made it this far in the book, you are one of those evolved souls who is ready to take the steps towards authentic self-love.

As adults, it is important for our spiritual growth to join a tribe or community of people that accept and support who we are in our authenticity. This will allow us to bring to awareness those shadow aspects that are parts of who we are without the fear of judgment or rejection. Our shadow aspects retain great wisdom. They are the traits we came in with and when expressed from a place of divine truth, they are valuable and lovable aspects of our soul.

# Chapter 11

## Healing and Integrating the Shadow Self

*"Like the lotus flower that is born out of mud, we must honor the darkest parts of ourselves and the most painful of our life's experiences, because they are what allow us to birth our most beautiful self. We need the messy, muddy past, the muck of our human life—the combination of every hurt, wound, loss, and unfulfilled desire blended with every joy, success, and blessing to give us the wisdom, the perspective, and the drive to step into the most magnificent expression of ourselves. This is the gift of the shadow"*

*~ Debbie Ford,*

The first step in healing and integrating the shadow self is to become aware that we have a shadow. It is nothing to be afraid of. It is just a part of us that feels inadequate and unlovable. These parts are innocent and worthy of love. They just do not feel that way. We do not see our shadow, but our shadow parts show up all the time, especially through our relationships with others.

The young boy whose father passed away can fear abandonment. His mother now must work double shifts to provide for the family. He feels alone as a child. This could show up in his adult life as a man who is non-committal. He may create a false identity that believes love ties him down and he wants to be a free spirit. What he is not saying is "Everybody I love abandons me." He will believe his false self represents his true desires. When he is unable to distract himself, or when he sees others in committed relationships, he may feel the pain of loneliness. He will quickly find a way to distract himself from those fearful thoughts. He is keeping his shadow self suppressed by not allowing any thoughts or feelings to surface that negate his free spirit attitude.

The little girl whose mother called her stupid most of her childhood will date only uneducated men. She has convinced herself that men with higher intelligence are arrogant and not her type. She is more drawn to the average uneducated man. This is her protector part making sure no one calls her out on her lack of intelligence. Although she may be a well-educated woman, the younger version of herself feels stupid and inferior to intelligent people. Her false self becomes the savior.

These may seem like normal behaviors because we cannot see that there are survival fears underlying these behaviors. We may trace these behaviors back to childhood, but if we logically try to resolve them without paying attention to the emotional pain and survival energy attached to them, then we are not healing the shadow self.

We can recall many challenging times in our lives, but the emotional pain we experienced could be absent from our recalled memory. When we experience emotional trauma, the survival brain kicks into full gear as the logical mind becomes dormant. We cannot be thinking logically while we are focused on a threat to our safety. We do what we can to fix the problem logically, without addressing the root cause of the problem.

The root cause of many unhealthy behavioral patterns is the feelings of unworthiness caused by the overwhelming emotions that were too much for us to process as children. If we help the inner child that is trapped in the shadows see themselves as worthy and deserving of love and, most importantly safe because the past is over, then we could help this emotionally undeveloped child part heal. This will put an end to the childlike reactive behavior, as the child part gets integrated into the whole self and becomes a part of that mature consciousness within the adult self.

As we heal and integrate our shadow parts, we become whole and balanced. This will allow us to have abundance in all areas of our lives. When we ignore these hurt parts of us, we become more attached to our false selves and our drive for acceptance. We may never get to know and love who we really are if we continue to fear our ability to be loved. We will continue to rely on the false self to gain love and acceptance by others. Although these deeply hidden fears of unlovability are outside of our awareness, they are always pulling on our energy and keeping us limited in our human potential.

Healing the shadow self can be accomplished with a therapist or anyone who specializes in inner child healing, parts therapy, or shadow work. It is not a complicated process, but it could be a sensitive one. There could be a pouring out of emotions that have been trapped in the body since childhood. This is like a cathartic release. The shadow healing process is one of the best ways to free the mind from old destructive thought patterns and release the body from emotional distress.

During a shadow healing process, there would be a compassionate dialogue between the wise adult self and the fragmented child self. This dialogue would include helping the child self see the bigger picture. The bigger picture includes an understanding of the adults in their life and how these adults are unknowingly acting out their childhood traumas. The child self, to complete their healing, must be aware that they are innocent, safe, and no longer a child. They must realize the divine truth - that they are loved and lovable. The only reason they did not feel that way growing up is because their primary caregivers did not feel love for themselves. This is not the fault of the primary caregivers. It is an ongoing issue of generational trauma that we need to address on a deeper level.

Once the child part realizes that the grown-ups in their lives were projecting fear instead of love because of their own unhealed trauma, then the child part can release themselves from their negative bond with their caregivers. This will release them from the trap of unworthiness that their caregivers unknowingly dragged them into. Once the child part feels their innocence, purity, and is ready to reconnect to their spiritual essence and divine truth, an integration can take place. The healing process will include authentic forgiveness by the adult-self for not realizing their value as a child and forgiveness of those that projected their pain onto the innocent child. This cannot be achieved superficially. The magic happens when authentic love is fully expressed. This is attained effortlessly if the healing takes place from a higher level of awareness. This means a better understanding of human consciousness and deeply felt compassion for human emotional suffering.

We can feel whole again, but first we must finish our unfinished business. This means we need to complete the past, so it does not keep seeking our attention. The only way to complete the past is to allow our shadow parts to come to a place of peace and a full acceptance of ourselves. The past cannot be resolved if we keep it below awareness, with parts of us hiding in the shadows as we give our power to the ego mind. We lose too much of our true selves doing that. We did not come onto this planet to hide in shame or pretend to be someone we are not. We came here to explore the material world through the consciousness of love and divine truth so we can show up in our authentic selves. When we entered this world, we did not know that this was our mission. We need to help those self-rejected parts of the whole self become aware of their goodness and their true spiritual power so we, as divine beings, can live like the miracles we are and do what we came here to do.

It is important to note that we are not expected to suddenly wake up one morning and find ourselves in full harmony and self-love. We are on this journey to find ourselves after losing ourselves. Our journey is about seeing our value no matter what we experienced in life. This will take some deeper healing work and the divine wisdom you came in with.

# Chapter 12

## Acceptance of Our Masculine and Feminine Energies

*'If any human being is to reach full maturity both the masculine and the feminine sides of the personality must be brought up into consciousness'*

*~ Mary Esther Harding*

As souls that hold both feminine and masculine energies, we share many of the same traits as our gender opposite. When these energies are balanced, we feel more like our true selves. The balance does not mean percentage. Each soul has its own natural balance that it came to earth with. If these energies go out of balance due to familial, cultural, or societal conditioning, then our energy body will be off balance.

Little girls were taught to be lady-like, play with dolls, and be pretty so they can catch a good man to take care of them when they grow up. Little boys were taught to be strong, unemotional and get a good education so they can financially support their wife and children when they grow up. Children have learned to adapt to these expectations to avoid rejection by society. This is old conditioning and usually does not apply to today's world, but some of these beliefs still linger deep within our minds.

Sometimes little girls like to jump in mud puddles, play football and may grow up to be the breadwinner in the family. Sometimes little boys have weak moments, need to express emotions and want to be in dance and theatre. It is now more globally acceptable to be your true self than it was for prior generations.

The feminine energy within the soul body is nurturing, creative, intuitive, empathetic, and gentle. The masculine energy within the soul body is strong, confident, rational, analytical, competitive, and independent. If we cannot allow ourselves to feel these parts of us due to fear of rejection, it will throw our energy out of balance. We need to embody these energies and be able to bring them forward as needed during our journey. If any of these traits become stifled, then it could cause feelings of disintegration. For example, if a new dad suppresses his nurturing energy due to the conditioning that the woman takes care of the children, not only would he lose out on the most precious moments of child-parent bonding but may feel a sense of emptiness in his soul. These are learned behaviors from witnessing familial patterns as children. The important thing is that we are evolving as a society and many of these old unhealthy human patterns are dissolving.

When masculine energies become suppressed, the male figure may not have the qualities for self-soothing when needed, may lack empathy, be disconnected from their creative inspiration, and may hold back tears to avoid shame or embarrassment.

If a woman needs to compete for something, but due to the conditioning that women who compete are not ladylike, she may suppress the energy she needs to succeed in life. For example, a woman wants to attain a higher-level position at her job but sees that there are several people competing for the same position. A part of her believes that being forceful and assertive about her professional qualities and abilities is unattractive so she remains modest and reserved during the interview. Her fear of being too masculine could keep her from advancing in the company. This can cause her to feel that she does not have what it takes to succeed, leaving her feeling inadequate.

We may have more creative energy than we do analytical energy or vice versa. It does not matter whether we are male or female in our physical structure. We embody both masculine and feminine energies and it is important that we do not limit our lives because we believe we must only express parts of ourselves in the real world.

Some people are still trying to balance these energies because they are still under the mind conditioning of their family.

We must give ourselves permission to express masculine traits if we are a woman and be able to express feminine traits if we are a male. Everything we express from within should hold a balance that comes from our authentic selves. This means not being overly sensitive or overly nurturing, which could be related to people pleasing or co-dependency. It also means not being overly independent or analytical which could relate to overcompensating for feelings of weakness or intellectual uncertainty.

Knowing our limits does not mean we suppressed some of our energy. By nature, the male anatomy in most cases would be physically stronger than the female anatomy. The female may be stronger in the mind than the male. When we look for balance, we are looking for our ability to tap into these energies when necessary, so that we do not become a helpless female or an unemotional male. This would indicate a lack of balance. We are strong, capable human beings with emotional energy. If we do not allow ourselves to claim our full potential, then we are causing our own feelings of deficiency. We are better and wiser than that, but we just got caught in the programming of our minds due to the rules and regulations that go against our divine nature.

# Chapter 13

## The Biggest Obstacle to Self-Love is Self-Rejection

*"Self-rejection is the greatest enemy of the spiritual life because it contradicts the sacred voice that calls us the 'Beloved'. Being the Beloved expresses the core truth of our existence"*

*~ Henri J.M. Nouwen*

Before we can understand the struggles to fully embody authentic self-love, first let us look at what self-love means.

Self-love is a unique journey for all of us. We all have different humanistic and spiritual needs. Self-love is honoring what is right for us and doing the proper things to keep our energetic field and physical structure balanced and duly protected from lower energies. Self-love is creatively blending our human and spiritual aspects to establish peace and harmony in our lives.

When we love ourselves, our priority is our well-being. We put the work into balancing our spiritual, emotional, mental, and physical bodies. We can give ourselves compassion, acceptance, nurturing, attention, spiritual healing, and rest when needed. We strive to be in tune with our physical bodies and at peace within our emotional state. When there is an imbalance in any level of our being, we make it a priority to bring ourselves back into balance.

Self-love goes beyond self-love affirmations, self-pampering, and external self-care. It is about ensuring that we are being honored and respected for who we are. We do not fluctuate between the false self and the true self. We remain in our truth and stay dedicated to our values, even when it is uncomfortable for others. We are aware when we need to wear a social mask. We are aware that in certain situations we may need to adjust our personality traits to avoid making others uncomfortable. We do not hide who we are, but we may not express ourselves fully during certain times out of respect for the emotional needs of others.

Self-love is being able to forgive ourselves for the times we forget about ourselves. We treat ourselves kindly even when we make mistakes. We are in touch with our humanness as well as our spirit. Self-love means remaining devoted to our purpose in life, regardless of the challenges we will face during our physical journey.

Self-love also includes seeing the divine essence in others as well as within us. When we see others out of balance, we do not take it personally. Self-love means seeing that their journey is for their soul's growth even if we do not agree with it.

Self-love is being able to set appropriate boundaries without guilt. It is speaking up for us when others are condescending, belittling or disrespecting our boundaries. It is seeking fairness in all situations that involve our time, space, energy, personal matters, material belongings or well-being. Self-love is saying no when we need to.

Self-love is loving all parts of ourselves. When we are loving only parts of us, but working on healing and integrating the other parts, then we are on a journey to self-love. This is good. This is where most of us are. We are on a journey to learn how to release ourselves from the opinions and projections of others and come back to our truth. We realize that life may never be perfect, but we are perfect in our true essence.

We cannot expect to jump into authentic self-love regardless of our experiences. Self-love comes from learning the lessons from these experiences, taking in valuable wisdom, and applying it towards our healing journey. When we take the time to heal our souls, release any blame towards others, and just focus on coming back into energetic balance, then we are moving closer to our divine truth. It is the awareness of our trapped emotions and our desire to work through them that will start us on our journey to authentic self-love. It is the lack of awareness that blocks our ability to evolve as souls, which keeps us stuck in old patterns, unresolved fears and survival consciousness.

If we are thriving in one level of our being, but failing in another without checking into the cause, then we are not in authentic self-love. Parts of us are in self-denial and self-sabotage. If we are keeping our spiritual body tuned into a high frequency by doing spiritual work but ignoring the health and wellness of our physical body, then our energies will not be balanced. When our energies are not balanced, somewhere there is a lack of self-love. Overcompensating in one level, but giving less attention to another level, is not honoring the whole self.

It is not easy to keep all levels of our existence in balance. It takes motivation, dedication, and a direction towards self-love. If we allow ourselves to stay out of balance, then we are not working towards self-love, but trapped in self-neglect. Self-neglect drains our energy and is an indication of self-rejection. This may trigger some people, but please be aware that you are worthy of the highest love and your Creator loves you no matter what. This is about you loving you. This is you realizing that you are an extension of the All-Loving Creator, but you have not fully embraced this divine energy. When you do, you will realize the divine miracle that you are. You will treat all parts of your being with the highest love, honor, and respect. You deserve to live in your full spiritual power and the only thing that holds you back is your lack of commitment to you. When you believed your true self was not enough, or too much, for those that cared for you during childhood, you shut down genuine parts of yourself. When you rejected parts of yourself to gain acceptance and feelings of belonging, it was a natural human response to fear. Now you are an adult with better coping skills than you had a child.

If we are not doing the inner healing work to balance our emotions, that is self-neglect. If we are not properly nourishing our physical body with foods that heal, balance, and strengthen, that is self-neglect. The same goes for our mental and spiritual bodies. Self-neglect is self-abandonment, which leads to self-sabotage.

Focus your attention on your thoughts. Do you need to say positive affirmations daily to counteract low-level thoughts that you choose to ignore? If so, then you may be fighting an internal battle of unworthiness. Are you spending time quietly meditating in an impatient energy? If so, then your nervous system may not be familiar with peace. Do you want to eat healthy, but keep reaching for unhealthy foods? You may be trying to feed emotional emptiness or distract yourself from negative thoughts.

It is important to check in with yourself and monitor all levels of your being for balance. We are not expected to stay perfectly balanced all the time. You are still human, and many things can pull you away from that space. The important part is that you do not stay too long in self-neglect. The balance of your whole-being must always take priority as an act of self-love. If outside circumstances are pulling you away for an extended period, check your priorities to make sure you are not putting your well-being at risk. Circumstances that pull us away are normal, but we need to stay determined to get back on track as soon as we can. This shows commitment and perseverance, which means you are self-aware, which is the initial step in your self-love journey. Maybe we are busy parents who are trying to balance career, family life, social life, and our personal needs. Life has placed many demands on us which could cause overwhelming stress as we try to keep up. We need to make our well-being the priority, so we have the energy to keep a steady balance. This is not a selfish thing. It is a self-love thing.

To show yourself some good authentic love, start with your mental body. Monitor your thoughts, actions, and inactions to see if they feel like self-love to you. Be aware of your interactions with others. Whenever you find yourself in situations that drain the energy body like incessant gossiping or insufferable complaining, find a way to excuse yourself to preserve your energy. Whenever someone is unkind, disrespectful, or unfair towards you, ask yourself "what would someone who loves themselves do in this situation," and then do that. Having the ability to walk away from anything that pulls your energy down shows a dedication to your well-being.

Next, check in with your emotional body. Are you feeling any uneasy sensations in your body? Are you living in the present moment, or do you keep going back to the past? Is anything a big trigger for you? Your emotional body can cause havoc on your physical body if not treated with love and kindness. This means giving your emotions the attention they deserve. When you experience negative emotions, remember that you are human. There are no bad emotions. Emotions are messengers and we must listen to them carefully with compassion and non-judgment. We can learn a lot about ourselves by understanding our emotions. If you find that you have negative emotions that take control over your well-being, then an act of self-love would be to seek out healing so you can come back into balance. Your emotions are important because they help you understand what you need to pay attention to.

Your spiritual body is just as important as the other levels of your being. If your soul goes too much out of balance, it will cause a disturbance in all levels of your being. Your soul body is your true essence. It is your divine energy body that is the source of self-love when not weighed down by painful memories. It loves you unconditionally and wants to enjoy this human experience from a level of unwavering faith and trust. If you are neglecting the needs of your energy body by being too distracted by the human experiences of fear and desire, then your soul will suffer, along with the rest of your whole self.

The energies from low-level thoughts and negative emotions burden the soul. When the soul becomes burdened, we look to outside sources to find balance. Sometimes this includes indulging in unhealthy practices that bring us temporary emotional comfort. This goes against our journey to self-love.

Our physical bodies are always speaking to us. All unbalanced energies will eventually settle there. This is where we can feel the true depth of our pain. It will show up in all kinds of physical disharmony. We can distract from mental and emotional disturbances, but the physical body will eventually let us know that something needs our attention.

It takes dedicated work to keep ourselves in energetic balance. We must be patient and kind to ourselves. We place so many unnecessary expectations on ourselves because we want to be acceptable to the world. This is not why we are here. We are here to spread love into the world so we can heal humanity and bring peace back to our planet. We must find a way to let go of our need for external validation and focus more on healing our wounds so we can fulfill our divine mission. We cannot keep wasting time and energy on petty things that mean nothing when it comes to our true divine power. We are soul warriors that forgot their courage and strength. We cannot let all these judgments and fears of others pull us down to a level of unworthiness. We did as children because we did not know better. We know better now so we can do better now.

We are all the same as a collective energy of light and love, but we are all different in our physical needs, personality traits and spiritual gifts. We must accept ourselves and others through each human challenge. We all deserve to be loved for who we are as divine beings on the same journey to self-love.

It is not easy going through these human experiences that cause us to question the purpose of our lives. So many people are suffering from a disconnect to their divinity, causing them to solely rely on their physical journey. When the physical journey keeps pulling us deeper into the pain of unworthiness, then it makes it harder to trust that there is more to life. We can follow all kinds of spiritual gurus for confirmation that we are perfect divine beings of love and light, but if we continue to close our hearts due to so many disappointing human experiences, then we are stunting our spiritual evolution.

What keeps us from fully experiencing self-love is our attachment to our traumas. As disconnected adults, we place the blame on those that did not meet our childhood needs. As children, we blame ourselves for not being worthy of getting our needs met. The inner conflict is so overwhelming that we find it best to stay in our daily distractions and keep pushing through life as we fight an internal battle. If we continue to ignore that there is lingering pain from an unresolved emotional past, then we will not be able to fully embody the spirit of self-love. We, as wise evolved adults, have the resources that our shadow aspects need to heal the pain caused by self-rejection, but we must be willing to do the work.

Self-love is about unrestricted love, acceptance, understanding and compassion for the whole self and others. We cannot be in a place of self-love as we judge others or think of them as lower than ourselves. We are all perfect divine beings, simply learning our spiritual lessons here on earth. Self-love includes love for all divine beings, whether in a physical body or on the other side. It is the knowing that we are all one in spirit and our individual souls are experiencing the physical world for soul evolution. We must support each other as we travel through the trenches of darkness to come back to the light that lives within us. That spark of light grows stronger as we heal and grow together.

We are always teaching and learning at the same time. Those that have not reached a level of awareness to reach their divine truth need more time to find their balance. We are not here to judge or shame anyone. We are here to lovingly support everyone on their journey. If their consciousness falls so low that they are difficult to be around, then, as an act of self-love, we must do our best to minimize our time with them. We can send them love from afar and pray for their souls to find the healing they need.

We are all so loved and so perfect. We are learning this as we continue our journey. Do not beat yourself up. Give your rejected parts some love and kindness. Thank your false self for keeping you safe. As you learn more about who you are, you will start dropping the mask. Until then, remember that the mask was applied for your safety. When you realize you are safe in your authentic self and that there is a whole universe of love and support watching over you, then you can stand firm in your spiritual power. You are worthy of all the goodness the world can offer. No one can steal your divine right to receive abundance. What others can do is cause you to question your self-worth. That is only if you do not know your intrinsic value.

As you step closer to authentic self-love, you may find yourself being more creative, more understanding, and more compassionate. You will notice that you take gentle and adequate care of yourself because you want to, not because you must.

We must appreciate the life we have been given and make it better by being true to ourselves. We may have memories of loss and pain from the past, but once we become more aware of how the journey works, then we will begin to see those memories as an opportunity to heal, grow, learn, and evolve as a whole being. Having gratitude instead of resentment will take us closer to self-love. If we are journeying towards self-love, then we are doing what we came here to do. We are blessed to be able to reach this higher level of awareness and understanding. Do not let the fears that are permeating the planet pull you into a trap of unworthiness. Remember who you are and start balancing your energies. You are absolutely loved.

# Chapter 14

## The Importance of Authentic Forgiveness

*"Forgiveness will not be possible until compassion is born in your heart"*

*~ Thich Nhat Hanh*

To fully embrace our journey to self-love, we will need to do some forgiveness work. This is the hardest part of the healing journey. When someone has wronged us and we feel it deeply, we may have a difficult time releasing the pain of feeling betrayed and disrespected. Many times, the emotional pain we experience as adults originated in childhood. If we experience an intense emotional charge in our adulthood because something feels unfair to us, then we are most likely re-experiencing unhealed emotional pain from the past. Many times, as children we felt like life was unfair and that adults have so much power over our lives. They may disrespect us, shame us, abandon us, neglect or abuse us and we can't do anything about it. This causes feelings of betrayal because we put all our trust into the people caring for us. We do not feel safe when we are not being treated with fairness, kindness, love, and respect. This gave us a feeling of disempowerment. These feelings of disempowerment that linger in the lower levels of the mind become intensified whenever we feel wronged as adults. What we do not realize is that we still hold resentment towards those in our childhood that we believe treated us unfairly. It always feels unfair when one person can overpower the other. As children, we were at the mercy of our caregivers. We felt so helpless because we had to accept their behavior towards us when we believed they were being unfair and overwhelmingly controlling.

Sometimes it is not our primary caregivers that keep us in resentment. It could be the school bully, the tyrannical sports coach or the dominating sibling. Whoever treated us unfairly still holds power over us if we are not able to stand up for ourselves. This causes us to become extremely resentful when we encounter others that do not show us respect. We are still not in our power because we have not healed the past with forgiveness. Forgiveness should primarily be directed at ourselves for giving up our power even though we had no choice as children. Then, to fully release any negative bond with the past, we can choose to forgive those that held power over us because we realize they were just acting out their internal feelings of disempowerment. This is portraying a mature mind and heart of compassion which is deeply healing for the soul. We will then need to build up our inner power and learn how to hold others accountable for any mistreatment towards us. This is how we evolve. We claim our right to be free of the unhealed pain of others. This can be done with a compassionate heart so we can remain in a positive state of mind because negativity only weakens the soul.

The common phrase "it's time to take back your power" simply means you are now the one in control of your life. The only way to regain our lost power is to forgive the situation and the people involved that caused us to give up our power and shrink in shame. When we forgive the root cause of resentment and any feelings of anger that might go with it, we will not feel easily triggered by people when they tend to treat us unfairly. We will have enough strength to stand up for ourselves in a mature, compassionate, but stern manner. Over time, as we continue to gain more internal power through the practice of self-empowerment, we will become stronger in our sense of self and see all negative situations as a call for love and compassion.

The way we have been taught to forgive is on a surface level because we are forgiving from the level of the conscious logical mind. We forgive based on reason, not from a feeling that comes from the heart. Forgiveness needs to come from a place of compassion and understanding. When we forgive from the logical mind, we have only forgiven ourselves or others from intellectual thought, not feeling. Since perceived wrongdoings trigger unhealed wounds, forgiveness is more than a logical remedy to the hurt we experience throughout our lives. People will tell us to brush it off, it is not worth the energy, let it go, or it has nothing to do with us. All this may be true, and we may understand this on the logical level, but the problem is that we are experiencing it from a deep wound within us. As children, our only concern was losing the love we needed from our caregivers or the acceptance we needed from society.

It has been said by many spiritual gurus that all forgiveness is self-forgiveness. This is true because we really do not have to forgive the other person. We only need to forgive ourselves for letting them cause us pain. In other words, we gave them our power by not resisting their unfair treatment towards us. The real power is in compassion, love and forgiveness. We can heal the original wound that caused us to cling to our feelings of resentment and empower ourselves with inner wisdom and understanding of human consciousness. This will make it easier to forgive ourselves in current situations where we feel wronged. For us to truly forgive another that made us feel bad, then we will have to draw on our innate compassion and see them as unable to do better because they are stuck in their own woundedness. It is not up to us to fix what they need to heal within them. It is our job to heal ourselves, so we do not get triggered and keep the negative energy in full force.

Trying to forgive ourselves while we still have childhood parts that feel unworthy is an arduous task. When things go wrong for us as adults, or people treat us unkindly, we may feel resentful, while at the same time feel like it is our fault for their mistreatment towards us. Children cannot forgive themselves. They tend to punish the parts of themselves that they believe are inferior. They do not have self-compassion which is necessary for self-forgiveness. They may even have bitterness or anger towards themselves for not having the ability or capacity to meet the demands of their caregivers. These childhood beliefs influence how we react or respond in adulthood when we feel disrespected or betrayed by another.

With authentic self-forgiveness, we are forgiving the parts of ourselves that got stuck in feelings of unworthiness because we did not realize our innocence and true value. Whenever our adult self gets triggered, it pulls this suppressed part of us into that familiar feeling of rejection, unlovability, and disempowerment. Genuine forgiveness is an act of self-love. Since most triggering reactions during adulthood come from the wounded inner child who may feel angry and resentful, logical forgiveness will not help us heal. This allows the pain of the perceived wrongdoing to linger within us and continue to get triggered.

If you are deeply triggered by those who do you wrong, then you will need to go deeper into your whole self to find the hook - the place in you that this person hooked into and opened a wound. If you are healed enough from past wounding, then you would be able to forgive yourself and others easier. This is because there would be no strong triggers. If you felt bad for a brief time, which is natural, the only forgiveness needed is self-forgiveness because you, in that moment, forgot that you have the wisdom, compassion and understanding that people are not living life from their true selves.

There needs to be a better understanding of human consciousness to achieve authentic forgiveness for the whole self and others. This cannot be achieved by the parts of you that are stuck in a time warp and do not have the level of consciousness of an adult. Before we can authentically forgive, we must be able to feel whole within ourselves. We would need to heal those parts of us that get triggered by hurt people who tend to hurt other people.

If you are not fully loving yourself, then those parts that you do not love, the parts you rejected that now live in your shadow self, will easily feel triggered by others. You will feel these emotional triggers in your physical body. This is because it is the nervous system that feels the jolt during a trigger which then signals the body to go into a survival response. In survival response, we will not forgive others because that would mean letting our guard down. As an adult, you are not trying to survive their unkindness. The pain and resentment come from an immature child's mind that is trying to gain acceptance and feelings of worthiness. When the hurt part is once again in a place of feeling rejected, it will only continue to shrink even more and put up a stronger guard. That guard is usually unhealed anger and resentment.

For true forgiveness to take place, we would need to be living through the aspect of Self. As mentioned above, we can think of Self as one who is whole and balanced because they have healed and integrated their shadow self. When this occurs, there will be no past hurts to trigger. There is self-love, self-respect, and self-acceptance. This means no matter what anyone says or does, you know you are always whole and deserving of love. You are also aware that you will not always receive love because many people are not yet capable of giving love. Self-love allows us to see the true intentions of others. Underneath their pain is someone who wants to be at peace with themselves and the world. If they cannot get to a place of peace, it is not because of anything outside of them. It is because they are in a fight within themselves. They live in self-rejection and fear. We place too much pride and ego on situations that cause disharmony within us. This is how we protect our wounds. What if we gave more love and compassion to ourselves whenever we feel betrayed or rejected? This will not be easy if we have parts of us that feel unworthy of love.

Forgiveness is also not easy if we do not feel compassion for the person we need to forgive. If we do not understand, from our heart space, that they are suffering inside, then we would have a challenging time feeling compassion for them. Their wrong doings would seem heartless and vicious, especially if they are triggering a deep wound within us. When we understand how pain can change the most innocent, loving soul and when we have a better understanding of human consciousness, then we will have compassion. We may even have compassion for those people who are so disconnected from love that they have hate for the world. We do not need to wish any suffering on people that are this lost because deep within their souls, they are already suffering. We just need to keep their energy at a comfortable distance so we don't experience pain through them.

Compassion is something we feel when we are whole within ourselves. When we are off balance and lack internal harmony due to fragmentation, we can become an easy target for those that project their internal pain onto others. The triggers could be quite painful because they come from the unhealed pain of a frightened child, not an adult. It is the child parts that are reliving the memories of feeling rejected. A child's reaction would be the same as if it were happening again. The adult mind knows that it is a different situation, but the child mind that lives within the adult self cannot tell the difference. This is because the child's mind is not logical, nor is it a person. The child's mind is a consciousness that is trapped in a bad memory where it cannot seem to escape. Therefore, compassion is necessary when the adult has reactive behavior. It is that child part expressing fear. If we can have compassion for any real time physical child that is hurting, then why do we lack that same compassion for our own inner child? It is because within our subconscious mind is the belief that we are deficient and undeserving of the love and respect we crave. We do not like this inner child and that is why we disowned these parts of us a long time ago. We do not like these parts of us because we believe they did not measure up to the expectations of our caregivers. As adults, these parts of us are still trying to meet the expectations of those we want and need in our lives. The remedy to releasing our need to please others to gain acceptance is a reconnection to this inner child through authentic compassion and forgiveness of self and others.

When you show compassion and forgiveness for an adult who is emotionally troubled and acts out with anger, then you are really forgiving their inner child. An adult does not act out, only a child does. An adult does not have temper tantrums, nor do they shut down during a crisis. These behaviors come from the unhealed inner child acting through the adult self. If we can remember this, we can view the adult as a child in need of love. This will help us show compassion towards them, which will lead to authentic forgiveness for both them and us.

We must acknowledge that most people have not healed their shadow self. This is what we need to understand so we do not take their actions personally. The best thing anyone can do for themselves is find enough self-love to do inner healing work, so they are not always being triggered by outside experiences. We are all innocent beings from the beginning. We become less kind, less compassionate and less loving as we go through the tough times in our lives. Our challenge have caused many of us to become more defensive, self-guarded and less forgiving. Then we may put on our persona of the kind, understanding person with people pleasing traits, not knowing that we are simply seeking acceptance and peace. This is the illusion of the mind and causes feelings of defeat, hopelessness, and sometimes the uncontrollable fear of rejection. The feelings of fragmentation that lie deep within us cause us to feel broken beyond repair. The truth is that we are not broken or unlovable; we only feel that way because of unhealed emotional trauma.

I would like to end this chapter by stating that authentic forgiveness and true compassion are the most crucial elements of our self-love journey. We need to believe in who we are as human beings learning what is meant by divine love. It is deep and profound and can only be experienced when we remember that our journey here is to discover this through our relationships with others. Without the challenges to love, we cannot learn about its value and healing power. To love is to have the compassion to forgive those that are still learning how to love. This includes those hidden, unseen and unacknowledged parts of ourselves.

# Chapter 15

## From Self-Awareness to Self-Love

*"The ultimate value of life depends upon awareness and the power of contemplation rather than upon mere survival"*

~ *Aristotle*

If our caregivers could not meet our childhood needs, then we must take the responsibility to make ourselves feel whole again. If we hold blame towards them, then we cannot take back control of our lives.

We naturally want to feel loved and cared for no matter what our age or what our life experiences have taught us. Whatever we needed and did not receive as children, we are still unconsciously seeking. We look to get our needs met through our adult relationships and mistake unhealthy connections as "normal" intimacy. The only way to have well-balanced connections with others is by loving ourselves first. If we did not have a healthy bond with our primary caregivers during childhood, then we will not have it in our adult relationships unless we are able to heal our internal emotional distress due to the lack of connection we felt in the past.

Loving ourselves first does not mean we must wait until we reach the level of unconditional self-love to be in a strong romantic relationship. We need only to be fully aware of our unhealed wounds and be actively working through the healing process. By healing our childhood wounds, we allow ourselves to become clear on what our needs are, and then we must take the necessary steps to ensure they are met in a healthy way.

The first step is to come to the unwavering conclusion that we deserve to get our needs met. Then we must accept that our primary caregivers did not know how to properly meet our needs. They were emotionally immature because of the emotional immature grown-ups that raised them. Although this seems unfair to us, our choice is to wallow in the pain of it or do something that will give us back our self-acceptance, restore the inner power of our true selves and ultimately allow us to embody that authentic self-love that has been hidden under the false self and the pain and fear of rejection.

As emotional beings, it is not always easy to release feelings of unworthiness if we have childhood memories of rejection haunting our minds. As children, we focused on earning the love of those we needed to bond with. As adults, we unconsciously believe we must earn love from others, so we neglect our own needs and adapt to the needs of those we want and need in our lives. This is what we did as children, and we continue to do it as adults without the awareness that the child in us is fighting for acceptance and safety. This builds anger and resentment, but at the same time gives us a false sense of security. The resentment and anger being felt in our adult relationships is from childhood memories when we could not get our needs met by our primary caregivers. We feel the neglect happening again, not realizing that we hold a hidden belief that we are undeserving of the love we seek. Any resentment is a clear indication that we still seek validation and a sense of worthiness. We want them to fix their inability to meet our needs so we can feel loved and safe. We may try to fix them ourselves and become irritated at their refusal or inability to change. If we do not become more self-aware, then we can get stuck in the "fixer" role, which will only become a frustrating and endless pursuit because we cannot fix anyone. We can only heal ourselves so we can release old patterns that negate self-love. When we choose ourselves, we are not looking to change anyone else. We are only looking to make the changes within ourselves which will bring us the loving, peaceful relationships we want, whether romantic or otherwise. Without self-awareness, we cannot acknowledge our survival patterns and, therefore, we will continue to pass on the responsibility of getting our childhood needs met through our adult relationships.

When we love who we are, we will ensure the fulfillment of our needs without giving up parts of ourselves in the process. When we are stuck in the past and trying to get our needs met through our intimate relationships, we may become resentful towards our partners. This is because they cannot meet all our childhood needs. It is not their job to do that. If we rely on them to make us feel whole, then we would be engaging in a co-dependent relationship with them. Co-dependency means having excessive emotional or psychological reliance on a partner so we can feel safe. When they fail to do that, we can become that angry or deeply depressed child again and hold them responsible for our painful feelings.

Not only do we need to be attentive to our needs and healing process, but we must ensure that our partner has or will do the necessary work, so they do not unconsciously seek healing through us, but with us. If we do not have the necessary awareness, then we will have a difficult time repairing any discord that may take place in the relationship. There is no love in this type of relationship. There are only fears, frustration, and a need for constant validation. We do not want to be in co-dependent, self-serving and ego-driven relationships. We want now what we needed as a child – unconditional love. The issue is that we keep looking to our intimate partners because they have replaced the disconnected caregivers from our childhood. This is why so many good relationships go bad. It is the survival patterns still trapped in our bodies, wanting to keep us safe from more harm. Every time a partner triggers us, we go into that familiar place of pain and fear. This will cause the child in us to employ a survival strategy that we found necessary as a child, but it may seem irrational as an adult. This can only cause more tension in the relationship. When we are in co-dependent relationships, the other person is also being triggered because they are stuck in their survival patterns. Neither person recognizes their part in the dysfunction within the relationship.

The most important aspect of being human is self-awareness. This is what will lead to self-love and healthier relationships. Without it, we are living through the false self which means stagnation in life and a whole lot of ego-tripping scenarios. There would be no emotional growth, either individually or within a unit, just a constant fight to get our needs, wants and desires satisfied. This is certainly not what we intended as our life mission. We are here to become self-aware, self-sufficient, self-loving, self-accepting, self-reliant, and most importantly self-chosen. When we choose ourselves first, we are letting the world know that we are ready for more honesty, integrity, and mature love to enter our lives.

If you want to truly honor yourself, it starts with knowing the higher truth. The only way to get there is by understanding how human emotions can lift us up or bring us to our knees as we beg for mercy. Many divine beings in their human forms have suffered a disconnect from their true selves. This has completely changed them, and they do not know how to bring their spirits back to life. Once they become totally lost in their fears, they focus on survival to the point of destruction of themselves and those around them. Their minds are experiencing life through a very dark distorted reality. If you have had close interactions with these deeply hurt beings, then you may feel traumatized by their projected fears. By holding them responsible to fix themselves or the past so you can be at peace is keeping you from creating your better future. Just because they did not have the ability to make themselves feel whole again does not mean you have to be stuck with them and their inability to see their divine value. Now is the time to choose yourself. This will prevent you from repeating the pattern of unworthiness that they became trapped in.

To set ourselves free from the past, we must understand it from a more loving and compassionate level. When we realize that these patterns can go back many generations, we will know that we are not the only ones that feel like victims. We will become aware that we are all victims of victims until someone stops the merry-go-round. It takes a strong person to do this because we are so conditioned to believe that choosing ourselves is a selfish act. We need to change that misguided belief for our own health and for the welfare of humanity.

We may have suppressed anger towards an alcoholic father who made us their punching bag. We felt unloved and unwanted. Our suppressed anger is due to our feelings of rejection and unworthiness. In our adult life, our anger continues to remain suppressed as our logical mind resents them for the inability to be the father we needed. What is not in play in this situation is the higher mind. The part of us that is a consciousness of love. The father got trapped in his pain of unworthiness and passes it onto his children. As adults who do not beat on our children believe that father should have had more control over his actions. Unfortunately, some people have become so mentally distorted due to their repressed feelings of unworthiness and deep-seeded anger that they lose control of their minds. The only way to heal from these unfortunate situations is to look beyond the issue with the compassionate energy of the higher mind. This is where authentic forgiveness takes place, and we take back our lives from those that had no control over their own.

We may already know from a logical standpoint that holding onto resentment keeps us from being at peace. If we know this, why can't we release the resentment? The reason is that we believe others have full awareness and control, so we become offended by their lack of consideration for us. The truth is, they would have more control if they did not fall into victimization and self-sabotage. When this happens, they cause feelings of victimization in others and unconsciously seek to bring them down to their level of pain. Although we may not be as dysfunctional as them, we might be projecting our energy of resentment onto those we care about.

Our primary caregivers did not have much help with their mental and emotional entrapments. This is why they were unable to hold a loving space for us. Although it was wrong of them to neglect our needs, mistreat us, emotionally or physically abandon us, control or restrict us to our detriment, we need to find a way to forgive ourselves for falling into their trap and taking on their baggage. We can also forgive them for not knowing how to see themselves as lovable, which kept them from knowing how to properly love us.

If we cannot expand our awareness to see the bigger picture around the people who cannot see their internal value, and instead resent them for falling short of our expectations, then we have unknowingly decided to match their consciousness instead of rising above it. So much of the physical journey is about knowing who we are no matter how wrong it went for us growing up. This is a difficult concept to grasp, especially when we are fueled with unresolved anger. It takes inner healing work to release this pain and let go of the unproductive patterns that we have become accustomed to. To live a life of peace, we must not carry resentment against those that cannot find love for themselves, which causes them to unconsciously project out nonlove towards others. If we can hold a compassionate heart for their internal suffering, which then led to our suffering, we can break the cycle of intergenerational trauma that has plagued our familial line. Although our pain did not start with us, it can certainly end with us. Not only will it bring us peace and allow us to be self-aware and self-loving, but we will also contribute more love and peace to the world, which is why we are here. It means we learned how to rise above the challenges of nonlove and seek the true purpose of our souls – the embodiment of love consciousness.

We may have deep feelings of anger buried below our awareness because a mother was depressed. Our memories from childhood feel like neglect and loneliness. We did not receive attention or affection from mom. We only have memories of her lying on the couch just staring at the ceiling. We had to fend for ourselves most of the time. We were embarrassed to bring friends to the house. As adults, we look back and label mom as a woman who was too emotionally unstable to be a mother which keeps us in resentment. As adults, we  may feel a sense of sadness as we recall memories of mom's inability to fight her inner battles. We do not realize the anger we are holding onto because we felt cheated out of our childhood and the motherly nurturing we craved. Deep within us are the feelings of unworthiness from not being good enough for mom's attention. As children, we do not understand depression, only our need for survival. We have adult logical understandings, together with hidden childhood emotions of resentment towards mom and feelings of unworthiness about ourselves. This is a cocktail of deep emotional pain for which there is no remedy without self-awareness. We will always be under emotional distress unless we realize that we must heal our suppressed emotional wounds before we can be at peace with ourselves and others.

Neither of the scenarios above are your exact situation, but they are examples of our humanness and the reason we stay trapped in our pain and unable to move towards authentic self-love.

As children, we could not see how the adults in our lives were drowning in their unhealed childhood pain and that their only outlet was medication. They did not know how to heal the mind, only how to block out the pain. Their pain became trapped inside of them way before we were born. This is what we must understand. We are not the cause of it. They are not the cause of their pain either. What we are all guilty of is lack of compassion that goes beyond the surface level. Although we are more evolved than those before us, we all still suffer from unhealed pain that most likely originated many generations before us.

Not getting our childhood needs met can cause deep hurt and distrust in the world. As children, we held back our sadness and anger to avoid further rejection. It is important to remember that our ability to push our emotions out of conscious awareness is a gift. The world is so scary and confusing when we are small. If we had to add in feelings of unworthiness, we would not be able to properly function in life. By suppressing our emotions, we were able to find some peace. As a child, you chose yourself through survival consciousness. You are now a grown-up. You must choose yourself again by seeing those unhealthy childhood patterns as no longer necessary for your survival. These patterns were your only life support when you were young. Now you are free to choose yourself in a whole new way. Your spirit (the true you) was forced into hiding as the false you (the ego mind) became your savior. When you revive that inner spirit, you come back to the real you. You become self-aware so you can see your true value and return to self-love. This will give that innocent you who suffered from the fear of nonlove and a better future filled with love and abundance.

Taking back control of your life means releasing others from the responsibility to make you feel whole again. Remember, you are not broken because you are spirit in your true self and spirit cannot be destroyed in any way. Your soul just feels fragmented from so much unhealed pain. The only way you can meet your own childhood needs, find happiness deep within you, and live a life of emotional stability is by choosing you from a higher level of consciousness. It is free from selfishness, self-pity, or self-preservation. It is you claiming your sovereignty as you take the journey towards authentic self-love.

Before we look to romantic partners for love and affection, we must feel it for ourselves. We may not feel completely healed, but we must see enough value in ourselves to heal and grow with our partner. If we are completely in denial of our wounding and only pretend to love ourselves, we will project our wounding onto our partner which will lead to a breakdown in the connection.

We can meet our childhood needs by first acknowledging what they are. Then we need to see how we can give ourselves what our primary caregivers were not capable of. The most important part of this work is removing all blame towards ourselves and others. This is what kept us from being self-aware. We had too many suppressed parts that held us in darkness and kept us from seeing the bigger picture in life. Once we take control of our own healing, then we can remind the younger version of ourselves that they are worthy of receiving the love and attention they craved as a child. It is the utmost important to express to the inner child that the people they needed to meet their needs were stuck in their own wounding and did not have the resources, knowledge, or strength to help themselves. This caused them to deny their pain and project it onto the innocent children they do love, and yet could not express it appropriately because their love for themselves and others became buried under their childhood wounding. This will help release the resentment and anger the inner child is holding onto. The true self of those that hurt us are only capable of love and compassion. If we could not experience their true selves, we must be self-aware enough to realize we were experiencing their false selves who is stuck in childhood survival consciousness and that is what caused our pain.

With a true understanding of human consciousness, it would be easier to release the past. Once we realize how difficult it was for our caregivers to meet our childhood needs, we will be able to release them from the obligation to be the caregivers we needed them to be. The reason it is easier for us to heal ourselves than it was for our ancestors is because we can express our pain without getting diagnosed by doctors as emotionally neurotic or psychologically dysfunctional. We also have many healing modalities that were not available to those who came before us. Ancient healing practices are now more acceptable and more prevalent. These modalities can help us reconnect with our inner child to bring them the love, affection, praise, and attention they need. A good facilitator can help us through our suppressed traumas, so we are no longer fighting against ourselves. Once we heal and integrate our innocent child parts, we will be able to continue our healing from a higher level of consciousness because we will be self-aware. The generations before us did not have much self-awareness. They lived their lives from their unconscious fears of unworthiness. This is not an excuse for unhealthy behavior, but it is a strong reason why we should not hold them accountable for our pain. They did not have enough awareness to see their own dysfunctional behaviors. We can only pray for them to heal so they can come back to their true selves. If they have crossed over, then we can pray that their souls find peace. Their caregivers caused them suffering, and then they caused us suffering. So much emotional pain has been endured by so many innocent souls because of lack of self-awareness and lack of self-love. We can be the generation that stops this cycle by having compassionate understanding and living by the higher truth.

We must have enough compassion in our hearts to see those hurt parts of us as valuable children whose spirit has been squashed due to feelings of nonlove. It is the light of spirit within us that is the truth of who we are. That is where our value is. To meet that internal spirit, we must come with an open mind and trusting heart. It is important to be aware of how the child's mind works so we realize that we need a loving, delicate approach when working with our inner child and their unmet needs. It is that inner child that lost contact with their spirit and developed defensive strategies to conquer their negative emotions.

We need to stop looking back towards our primary caregivers for some kind of explanation as to why they could not meet our needs. This will keep us stuck in the past. You are the one you need now. Do not turn your back on yourself. There is no denying that many of us have had some awful experiences growing up. If we keep victimizing ourselves, then we will always be the victim. Instead, imagine yourself as the hero you have been waiting for. See yourself in your strengths instead of being weakened by the fears of unworthiness. That is a trap and you have to be strong enough to release yourself from it.

We cannot expect ourselves to suddenly know how to receive what we did not receive our whole lives. We must learn how to nurture ourselves back to feelings of wholeness. This means doing inner work to find out where we feel lack. Are we people pleasing to gain friendship, love or belonging? Do we know how to set boundaries? Can we allow affection and intimacy into our lives? When we speak, are we being heard? Can we validate ourselves instead of seeking validation from others? Can we empathize with others when they are suffering? Can we accept ourselves for who we are? These are all the questions we need to ask ourselves. This is how we can check in with ourselves. Most importantly, can we offer ourselves unconditional love?

If we continue the same cycle that our caregivers got trapped in because they lacked self-awareness, then we have given up our divine right to be free of emotional burdens. If we pity ourselves for our loss of love and attention during childhood, we become less inclined to meet our own needs. We get stuck in the trap of "woe is me and I can't change that." We deserve better. Our caregivers deserved better. We all got caught up in the fear trap. That was not the true mission.

We have evolved higher than the generations before us. We still feel some disconnect to our true selves because of the trauma we absorbed from our families. We became too dependent on proving our worth as a survival source. This will keep us under the watch of ego when we should be under the loving guidance of our higher selves. It really is a delicate balance when we are trying to live a safe and healthy physical life, while we stay true to our divine essence. As you can see by the disharmony in the world, many people have not found the right balance. The question is: can you be the one that levels up, takes the reigns, and go full force into your spiritual power? It will not be easy, but there is no one stopping you, except you. You need to decide if you are worth the effort. Can you say "yes, I am worth it" and get back on that journey to self-love? If so, the next question might be "where do I start?" We start with self-awareness. This means seeing how we unknowingly keep the ancestral survival patterns alive and how we can return to the true healing source which is self-love.

# Chapter 16

## Your Journey to Self-Love is Now

*"As I began to love myself, I found that anguish and emotional suffering were only warning signs that I was living against my own truth"*

*~ Charlie Chaplin*

From the moment of conception until this very day, there is nothing in this physical world that can take from us our divine value. No matter how our experiences have shaped our perceptions, personalities, and the way we navigate our journey, we must always know there is one way to self-love and that is through the higher truth. Your self-love journey has always been in the now moment. You are always learning lessons that lead you to self-love. The lessons you did not learn will keep repeating through different events to give you the opportunity to raise your vibration by resolving the barriers to self-love. Authenticity is the goal, but the self-love journey is what leads you there. Our personal spiritual guidance from our higher selves is taking us through the steps of evolution, and we are not lagging. We are in a good place energetically and realize that those prior versions of ourselves did not know how to heal so we should never hold them in shame, and just be grateful for their part in our evolution process

The truth is that our value as spiritual beings in physical bodies is not measured by how we are treated by others on this journey with us. We are the consciousness of love that has forgotten our worth because we fell into the lower consciousness of fear. There is nothing stopping us from releasing old cyclic patterns that keep us trapped except our own minds. We can live more from the higher mind where our inner spirit connects to all that is divine love, or we can stay in the lower mind where we keep fighting for acceptance. It is not a difficult choice, but it can be challenging to shift our thoughts into a higher frequency if these thoughts have caused us to believe we are stuck.

We are currently living through a global transformation. We can either jump on the train towards ascension or be held back because of our inability to see the higher truth. Ascension only means we are shedding the false self that was created by the fears that permeate this planet. It does not mean we are moving into higher consciousness. We are already higher consciousness. We are releasing all the barriers to it so we can embrace our divine truth and ascend out of the trap. We can only be defeated by the past if we do not make the effort to see beyond it and raise our awareness higher than the problems we faced on our journey. If we are living life through the lower levels of the mind, where we keep repeating the past in an unconscious effort to fix it, then we will miss our ride to greater love for ourselves and the world. You are being called to act now. You have the support of those who have made the choice to live by this higher truth. They have decided to stop chasing love and just embrace who they are as love consciousness. They are self-aware and realize they can trust the process of returning to self-love by letting go of what is blocking it.

We are being birthed into a whole new world. We are not physically leaving the planet, but we are energetically rising by releasing the burdens of pain that keep us from seeing our worth. You can probably feel the chaos around you as the shifting can be tumultuous at the beginning, but there will be smooth sailing as we progress. This is an extremely exciting time. Do not fall short because you believe you are too spiritual to worry about an unhealed past. We are all spiritual beings. We are all divine. We are all made in the image of the All-Loving, All-Knowing Creator. Saying affirmations and posting self-love memes on social media without self-awareness is futile. You must honestly know who you are without the mask. If you have not healed and integrated the parts of you that are in hiding, then you will not fully ascend out of the unworthiness trap – only parts of you will. Those hidden parts will be left behind in the lower energies of fear. That means you are leaving behind a part of your soul – the innocent, lovable, child in you that feels fragmented from the whole self. That is unfair to you. You deserve better. Although these hidden parts of you are already part of the higher consciousness, they are not self-aware, so they remain in lower consciousness, held back by self-rejection.

We have all be greatly challenged in earth school, some more than others. If we keep allowing the past hurts to control our future, then we have given up our free will and our divine right to live a harmonious life. Doing inner healing work is an absolute necessity. It shows that you love yourself enough to find and heal the issues that keep you from seeing your worth. We are not meant to stay trapped in the ego mind. We must have gratitude for its purpose, but we must also take back the power we gave it a long time ago. It is keeping us from loving all parts of ourselves. It does not realize that its outdated protective strategies are not working for us anymore. It is time to fully grow and evolve.

Imagine yourself as a newborn baby. You came here to learn what it feels like to forget who you are so you can appreciate who you are. Somewhere on the journey you forgot about this miraculous being of love that came to planet earth through another soul in a human body. What a miracle that is. There is so much to be thankful for, but we will not have gratitude if we continue to focus on what we needed but did not receive. We cannot live in self-pity, self-blame, or self-rejection when we are meant to embody self-love. We are whole beings of love, light, and divine energy – we are spirits of love consciousness that can shift this planet into the vibration of the highest love if most of us conquer our earthly fears. We must take back our spiritual power and help others do the same. We are already whole, but life has caused us to feel shattered beyond repair. With the love of your divine self, you can bring the pieces together, so you feel complete within yourself and be one of the contributors towards a better world for all.

Life is not always fair. Some people have a much easier journey than others. It is unfair to say that you would be able to release all your pain if you suffered so much of it. That is why this is a journey. We are here to learn how to love ourselves through our pain. There are stories of people who have suffered greatly and found inner peace by connecting to their divine truth. They realized that they cannot change their past. They found the strength to rise above the lower consciousness that has trapped them in fear and let the past be a lesson about the value of self-love. This is the strength many of us need so we can step into our self-love journey with pride and determination. We can look back at the many experiences that challenged us and see that we are still striving for self-love. Now is the time. We are more ready now than ever before. This is because we are in an ascension period. We are being called to collectively stand in our divine power. We can only do this if we love ourselves enough to release what is holding us back.

Your journey to authentic self-love is now. Are you ready to begin the process of loving all of you?

# Chapter 17

## Your Self-Love Checklist

*"Our first and last love is self-love"*

*~ Christian Nestell Bovee*

To embrace self-love is to be aware of the reason you question your lovability. It is not because someone treated you badly, it is because their treatment of you became your identity. No one can change your divine nature. Your identity is not your experiences. What you came here for is to learn from each experience so you can see the greatness in you. If you forgot your value, it is because the journey became too difficult for you to stay on course. That is the common theme for most of us. Now you are ready to meet those challenges head on using the power of your higher mind. That is where all your genuine love and compassion reside. If you would rather meet your challenges with anger and resentment, then you will stay in that energy and suffer the consequences until you see the lesson in it and apply it towards your spiritual growth.

You can choose your destiny now. Either stay trapped in the fears that invade this planet or rise to the level of your true divine self and embody that consciousness of love. I know it is not easy to just flip the switch. It takes work. The question is: do you love yourself enough to do the work?

You are an amazing gift to this world. You have so many untapped spiritual abilities. Every cell of your being will feel the flood of love consciousness running through you once you remove the blockages. Those blockages are strong because you made them strong. You can lovingly release them now. They did their job to protect you. You do not need those old survival patterns anymore.

You know who you are. As a divine being of light, you are invincible. You can show up in the physical world as the miracle that you are. You do not need anyone's permission to be you.

The questions below are for you to answer from a level of self-awareness and self-compassion. Before you answer the questions, tap into a higher level of consciousness through your choice of meditation. Choose one that relaxes your mind enough for you to let your answers surface from your innate wisdom. If your mind does not relax enough, your answers may come through from the ego mind. This will hinder your progress because you need to be in the higher levels of love and compassion to tackle some of these long-held beliefs that your subconscious mind does not want to release. These are the beliefs you survived on. Be patient with yourself and let the process unfold naturally. Be grateful that you have a strong mind and were able to save yourself from the wraths of emotional distress that you had to endure over the years. What amazing strength we all carry to keep ourselves intact during this difficult human journey. This means you are more than capable of stepping up now into your true divine power. Although at times you may have felt weakened, you were always growing stronger. You are simply shifting your strength from survival to embracing the love consciousness that you are.

You can also use a simple form of self-hypnosis by closing your eyes, taking a few deep breaths in, exhale slowly into your heart space to connect with your body, and count backwards from 10-1, as you softly say the words "deeper relaxed." This method will help you get out of your analytical mind and into the deep feelings held in your body.

Your answers to the questions below will help you gauge where you are on your self-love journey. It is all right if you are new to loving you; many of us are. Remember, it is a journey. The most important part of it is that you want to come back to you and are ready to do the work to begin the process of shedding the false you so you can come back to the true you. You got this! Do not forget the power of spirit that lives within you.

Use a sheet of paper to go through this self-awareness process. Sometimes, it takes several times to really grasp the meaning of being aware of your inner thoughts. The more you write the truth from your higher mind, the more you let go of the patterns that bind you.

Throughout this process, always remind yourself that this is a learning process. There is no wrong answer or time limit for completion of your inner healing journey. Just know that you are on the journey, you are the embodiment of divine love, and you are a miracle no matter what you have experienced.

1.      I question my lovability because:

Answer:

From my higher awareness, what I now know to be true is:

Answer:

2.      Others have caused me pain that lingers within me because:

Answer:

From my higher awareness, what I now know to be true is:

Answer:

3.      Things that trigger me are:

Answer:

From my higher awareness, what I now know to be true is:

Answer:

4.      I hold myself back from happiness because:

Answer:

From my higher awareness, what I now know to be true is:

Answer:

5.      I try to get my unmet needs through:

Answer:

From my higher awareness, what I now know to be true is:

Answer:

6.      The people that hurt me the most in the world are:

Answer:

From my higher awareness, what I now know to be true is:

Answer:

7.      I always placed my value on:

Answer:

From my higher awareness, what I now know to be true is:

 Answer:

8.  The part of my life where I experience lack is:

Answer:

From my higher awareness, what I now know to be true is:

 Answer:

9.  I blame others for:

Answer:

From my higher awareness, what I now know to be true is:

Answer:

10. What I needed that my primary caregivers did not provide is:

Answer:

From my higher awareness, what I now know to be true is:

 Answer:

11. When I look in the mirror, I see:

 Answer:

From my higher awareness, what I now know to be true is:

Answer:

12.     When I touch my heart, I feel:

Answer:

From my higher awareness, what I now know to be true is:

Answer:

13.     My worse memory as a child is:

Answer

From my higher awareness, what I now know to be true is:

Answer:

14.     I have suppressed the emotions related to:

Answer:

From my higher awareness, what I now know to be true is:

15.     My true values are:

Answer:

16.     The ways I can meet my own unmet needs are:

Answer

17.    The ways I can support my self-love journey are:

Answer:

I know, from my higher mind, that I am:

Answer:

As you heal the wounds of the past and become more self-aware so you can embrace the self-love journey with ease, say all of some of these affirmations first thing in the morning and again before you go to sleep. These are the times when your conscious ego mind is relaxed enough to allow the affirmations to sink into the lower levels of the mind where you have buried negative emotions from childhood.

My Daily Affirmations:

---

I see me now.
I choose me now.

---

I am ready to define my true values, meet my unmet needs and honor the spirit I am.

---

It is in my spiritual power to see above all problems and resolve them with self-love.

---

I trust that my true self is enough for the world. I no longer need a mask to hide who I am.

---

Even though I did not get all my childhood needs met, I am still and always will be a perfect divine being having a human experience.

---

In my physical space I am always a divine light no matter what is happening in my life.

---

I do not have to prove my worth to anyone. I know who I am and that is enough.

---

I give love and respect to all living beings and therefore the same shall return to me.

---

I find peace and harmony within my own light. I do not need to draw energy from others.

---

My life is complete because I am complete.

---

There is no greater power than Love and I embody it in its unwavering strength.

---

No matter how difficult things get for me, I stay peaceful, calm, and relaxed.

I see myself and all others in the likeliness of the Creator.

My spirit is bigger than any problem in my third-dimensional reality.

I live and breathe each day like the miracle I am.

Let me close this book with love from my soul to yours. I am on this journey with you, and I honor you as a sacred being of love and divine value. I know we have all been greatly deceived on this journey because of all the wounding that lingers from the generations before us. Some of them have strayed so far from love and could not find their way back. We are the chosen ones and must step into our mission now. We must lead the way back to self-love as a collective.

Let us not forget how powerful we are as a united body of love. We are the miracles that have come here to create change. It starts with us and then we spread all that love where it is most needed. The world is waiting.

We got this!

May You Always Feel Blessed By the Light and Love Within You.

Love and Peace

# **About the Author:**

Kelly Tallaksen is a Board-Certified Hypnotist under the National Guild of Hypnotists (NGH), an NGH Hypnosis Instructor, teaching basic and advanced hypnosis courses, President of the NGH Long Island Chapter, Published Author, Public Speaker on Human Consciousness and its Effects on the Soul and the Co-Producer of the short film "The Voice of Spirit", set to release in 2024.

Kelly specializes in transpersonal hypnosis, which is working beyond the physical realm to help her clients heal soul traumas that cause a disconnect to self-love. Kelly holds a PhD in Holistic Life Counseling, a Doctorate Degree in Metaphysical Hypnosis and is also trained in Holistic Psychology, Parts Healing & Integration, Age Regression, HeartMath™, Shadow Coaching, Ancestral Healing and Spiritual Healing Journeys. Kelly is the author of the published books *"The Voiceless Soul"* and *"Healing Our Unhealed Parts"* and several published articles about healing on a soul level.

Kelly has been a guest on several podcasts, internet TV and radio shows, sharing her wisdom, insight and expertise on healing through trancework to bypass the protective ego mind and heal on a soul level. Kelly contributes much of her understanding of human consciousness and the challenges of self-love through her work with clients who have shared so much of their inner self and the pain they hold within for the sake of acceptance by the world. Kelly's hope is to help people see their innate value no matter how difficult and challenging their human experience was, so they can express themselves authentically and live life like the miracles they are.

Kelly's work has been credited by many health and wellness institutions. She has received recognition awards from The International Association of Top Professionals as top professional in her field, The Herald Community as Long Island Businesswoman of the Year and Who's Who in America for her commitment and dedication to her work.

Kelly's hope is that you, as the reader of this book, see your true value as both human and spirit learning how to navigate this physical journey from your spiritual intelligence so you can fully embody self-love and spread that love and light onto planet Earth. As you learn how to face your own challenges with self-love so they can be resolved through the wisdom of the higher truth instead of challenged through ego and fear, you are contributing so much light to the darkness that hovers over this planet. You are helping to awaken humanity so they can embrace their divine truth. You are simply a miracle, so live your life in that truth.